GLOBETROTTER™

Travel Guide

The
PHILIPPINES

NIGEL HICKS

NH

NEW
HOLLAND

NEW
HOLLAND

★★★ Highly recommended
★★ Recommended
★ See if you can

First published in 2000
by New Holland Publishers (UK) Ltd
London • Cape Town • Sydney • Auckland

10 9 8 7 6 5 4 3 2 1

24 Nutford Place
London W1H 6DQ
United Kingdom

80 McKenzie Street
Cape Town 8001
South Africa

14 Aquatic Drive
Frenchs Forest, NSW 2086
Australia

218 Lake Road
Northcote, Auckland
New Zealand

Reproduction by Hirt & Carter (Pty) Ltd, Cape Town
Printed and bound in Hong Kong by Sing Cheong
Printing Co. Ltd.

Although every effort has been made to ensure
accuracy of facts, telephone and fax numbers in this
book, the publishers will not be held responsible for
changes that occur at the time of going to press.

Cover: *A colourful Jeepney, Philippines.*
Title page: *White Beach, Boracay Island.*

Commissioning editor: Tim Jollands
Manager Globetrotter Maps: John Loubser
Editors: Mary Duncan, Thea Grobbelaar,
        Peter Duncan
Picture researcher: Rowena Curtis
Design and DTP: Eloïse Moss
Cartographer: Carl Germishuys

CONTENTS

1
Introducing the Philippines

The Philippines is a sprawling tropical archipelago of over 7000 islands, stretching from close to Borneo in the southwest almost as far as Taiwan in the north. Most of the larger islands are mountainous with numerous volcanoes, a reflection of the country's location on the **Pacific Ring of Fire**. Many of the smaller islands are the tops of coral reefs, and some are low-lying, ringed by the spectacular white beaches for which the country has become famous. Beneath the waves are extensive coral reefs that both protect the shore from storms and provide a home to a wealth of marine life.

It is this natural beauty that draws people to the Philippines. The principal attraction is the tiny island of **Boracay**, with its stunning white beaches and azure sea, but there are other beach resorts that draw their share of visitors, such as **Puerto Galera**, **El Nido**, and **Panglao Island**. The country is also becoming one the world's great **diving** centres, with some magnificent reefs now accessible, especially those close to the beach resorts.

Inland, many visitors head up into the mountains of northern Luzon, known as the **Cordillera Central**, particularly to the city of **Baguio** and the rice terraces around **Banaue**.

Historical interest hinges mostly around the remains of Spain's 350-year colonial rule. There are several beautiful **churches** from this period, and in addition there is **Intramuros**, the old walled section of the capital city, Manila, and **Vigan**, an almost intact Spanish town that was once the capital of the far north.

TOP ATTRACTIONS

*** Boracay: spectacular beaches and resort facilities.
*** Alona Beach: good facilities, excellent diving.
*** El Nido: sheer cliffs and isolated beaches.
*** Sagada: mountain village surrounded by pine forest, with caves and scenic landscapes to explore.
** Puerto Galera: several beaches, world-class diving.
** Camiguin: beautiful scenery, an active volcano, hot and cold springs, and extremely friendly people.
** Banaue: spectacular mountain-side rice terraces.

Opposite: *Ancient rice terraces in the Cordillera Central mountains.*

Above: *Sabang beach in Palawan is just one of the Philippines' great beaches.*

> **GEOGRAPHICAL FACTS AND FIGURES**
>
> **Total land area:** 300,000 km² (115,200 sq miles).
> **Number of islands:** 7107
> **Principal islands:** Luzon (105,708km²; 40,592 sq miles); Mindanao (95,600km²; 36,710 sq miles); Visayan Islands comprising Panay, Negros, Cebu, Bohol, Samar, Leyte and Masbate (total area: 61,077km²; 23,582 sq miles); Mindoro (9736km²; 3759 sq miles); Palawan (11,785km²; 4550 sq miles).
> **Length of coastline:** 36,289km (21,773 miles)
> **Highest mountain:** Mt Apo, 2954m (9689ft).
> **Active volcanoes:** 22
> **Largest lake:** Laguna de Bay, 927km² (356 sq miles).
> **Area of coral reefs:** 34,000km² (13,128 sq miles)

THE LAND

The Philippines is situated on the eastern edge of Asia. It is bounded to the west by the South China Sea and to the east by the Pacific Ocean. Its nearest neighbours are the Malaysian province of Sabah and the Indonesian territory of Kalimantan, both on Borneo to the southwest. Across the South China Sea, about 1000km (620 miles) west, lies Vietnam, and a similar distance to the east are the Palau Islands. China lies about 500km (310 miles) to the north.

The Islands

Officially, the Philippines consists of 7107 islands, with a land area of almost 300,000km² (116,000 sq miles). There are six major island groups. The largest and most densely populated is **Luzon**, which forms the bulk of the northern landmass and is the site of the capital, Manila. **Mindanao** is the second-largest island, forming the southern landmass. Between is a cluster of islands collectively called the **Visayas**, principal of which are **Panay**, **Negros**, **Cebu**, **Bohol**, **Samar**, **Leyte** and **Masbate**. The fourth region is **Mindoro**, a mountainous island in the southern underbelly of Luzon. Southwestwards towards Borneo is **Palawan**, a long, thin, pencil-like island. Finally, in the far south, are the **Sulu Islands**, running from the western tip of Mindanao to within just a few kilometres of Borneo.

Coasts and Seas

With such a large number of separate islands, the Philippines has an incredibly long coastline, totalling 36,289km (21,773 miles), even longer than that of the United States of America. The highly indented coast has created 60 natural harbours and there are about 34,000km² (13,128 sq miles) of **coral reefs**. Beyond the reefs, the seabed around most of the islands plunges away to great depths even within the closely confined waters of the Visayas. Off the Pacific coast the seabed drops into the Philippine Trench, which just east of Mindanao reaches a depth of about 10,500m (34,450ft).

Mountains and Volcanoes

The Philippine islands are the tips of submerged mountains driven up from the seabed by the impact of the Eurasian and Philippine **tectonic plates** grinding against one another. Most of the resulting mountain chains are orientated north–south, and are subject to **earthquakes**. One of the most devastating in recent times occurred in 1990, seriously damaging the cities of Baguio, Dagupan and Cabanatuan, resulting in 1600 deaths.

The Philippines has over 200 **volcanoes**, 22 of them active. The country's highest peak, **Mt Apo**, is an inactive volcano. The country's most active volcano is **Mt Mayon**, known to have erupted 44 times. Towering over the city of Legaspi, it is famous for its almost perfect cone. South of Manila is a cluster of volcanoes, two of them active. The most dangerous – despite being one of the world's smallest volcanoes – is **Taal**. It sits on a small island in the midst of a lake that is said to be itself the caldera of a once huge volcano.

RING OF FIRE

The Philippines sits on the Ring of Fire, an arc of volcanoes that encircles much of the Pacific Ocean and includes Indonesia, the west coasts of North and South America, Russia's Kamchatka Peninsula, and Japan. These are all areas where several of the earth's major tectonic plates converge and grind against one another. In the case of the Philippines, the volcanic and seismic activities are caused by the small Philippine Plate pushing against the huge Eurasian Plate.

Below: *Mt Mayon is renowned for its perfectly conical shape, permanently smouldering crater and frequent eruptions.*

Climatic Variation

Weather patterns, divided mainly into wet and dry, are complicated by relative exposures to the southwest (from June to October) and northeast (from November to May) monsoons. Generally, areas exposed to the former are wet from June to October, and those to the latter are wet from November or December to January or February. Some areas will be wet at both times, though usually only to a moderate degree. All areas are at their driest in April and May, but these are also the hottest months.

Climatic Zones

Long dry season Nov–May
Intense rain Jun–Oct

Short dry season Mar–May
Moderate rain Jun–Feb

Rain falling during most of the year
Period of maximum rainfall Nov–Feb

No clearly defined dry season
Period of maximum rainfall Apr–Sep

No pronounced wet or dry seasons

PACIFIC OCEAN

SOUTH CHINA SEA

LUZON

MINDORO

SAMAR

PANAY

PALAWAN

CEBU

LEYTE

N

NEGROS   BOHOL

0   200 km

0   100 miles

MINDANAO

Below: *A footpath balances atop a tiny dyke in a rice field.*

The most notorious of Philippine volcanoes is **Mt Pinatubo**, situated in the Zambales Mountains, north of Manila. After lying inactive for 450 years, in June 1991 it produced one of the world's largest eruptions of the 20th century, devastating Central Luzon and killing hundreds of people.

Climate

The Philippines is a tropical country, whose weather is determined by the **southwest** and **northeast monsoons**. The former, blowing from June to October or November, brings heavy rain, while the latter, from November or December to May, tends to be drier, bringing rain mainly to just the exposed east coasts. The country is divided into five **climatic zones**,

more or less reflecting relative exposure to these monsoons. Thus, much of the west, including Manila, is very wet from June to November and dry for the rest of the year. Areas open to the northeast monsoon will be wet from December to March. Only in April and May is dry weather certain across the whole country, but these are also the hottest months.

Severe storms known as **typhoons** sweep across the northern half of the country from May to December (usually about 20 per year), travelling in a westerly or northwesterly direction, wreaking havoc on the eastern coasts and causing floods in Manila. Such storms do not affect the southern half of the country.

Plant and Animal Life

The Philippines has one of the world's highest **bio-diversities**, with an extraordinary range of plant and animal species, many **endemic**, or unique, to the country. Thus, 43 per cent of the country's birds and two-thirds of its mammals and higher plants live nowhere else. The reason for this enormous diversity lies mainly in the country's longheld isolation. With the exception of Palawan, the Philippines has not been attached to the Asian landmass in recent geological times. Thus, while Palawan received an influx of animals and plants from Borneo, those in most of the country evolved in isolation, producing quite unique forms.

UNIQUE WILDLIFE

The Philippines' isolation has ensured that a wealth of unique wildlife has developed. Hunting and loss of habitat have ensured that almost all are endangered. Some of the best known are as follows:

Mammals

Tamaraw: a form of wild cattle.

Philippine tarsier: one of the world's smallest primates.

Cloud rat: a large rodent; several species exist.

Golden-crowned flying fox: the world's largest fruit bat.

Bearded and warty pigs: several species exist in different parts of the country.

Philippine spotted deer: survives only in the Visayas.

Birds

Philippine eagle: the world's second-largest raptor.

Tarictic hornbill: several species exist in different parts of the Philippines.

Palawan hornbill: lives only in Palawan.

Philippine cockatoo: lives in several remote areas of the country.

Palawan peacock pheasant: lives only in Palawan.

Other

Philippine or Freshwater crocodile: survives in several parts of the country.

Above: *A gorgonian sea fan clings to a vertical wall in the deep clear seas around Tubbataha Reef Marine National Park, a remote atoll in the Sulu Sea.*

Plant life revolves mainly around the **tropical rain forest**, with **dipterocarp** trees, the tall giants of the forest, dominant in the lowland forests, and smaller tropical **oaks** taking over at higher altitudes. Below the tree canopy grow several species of pandanus, rattan, palms, vines and ferns. In the muddy estuaries and bays **mangroves** are quite common.

Coral reefs occur below the low-tide mark, with approximately 400 species of coral recorded in the Philippines. Healthy reefs are home to hundreds of species of fish, from the tiny striped **clownfish**, beautiful **butterflyfish** and **Moorish idols** to the huge **grouper**. Around the reefs that are surrounded by deep water it is common to encounter **barracuda**, **tuna** and **sharks**. In the deepest waters there are often **dolphins** and **whales**.

Many of the land animals are unfamiliar to visitors, although **macaques** are common. Palawan has a number of species familiar in other parts of Asia, such as the

PROTECTED AREAS		
The Philippines' 12 most important (for conservation value) protected areas are as follows:		
Protected area	**Location**	**Habitat**
Mt Apo Natural Park	Southern Mindanao	Rain forest
Mt Kitanglad Range Natural Park	Northern Mindanao	Rain forest
Northern Sierra Madre Natural Park	Northern Luzon	Rain forest
Subic–Bataan Natural Park	Central Luzon	Rain forest and mangroves
Mt Pulag Natural Park	Northern Luzon	Pine and mossy forests
Mt Kanlaon	Negros, Visayas	Rain forest
Siargao Island Protected Landscapes and Seascapes	Northern Mindanao	Rain forest remnants, mangroves, coastal scenery
Batanes Islands Protected Landscapes and Seascapes	Northern Luzon	Coastal cliffs and rocks, rain forest remnants
Agusan Marsh Wildlife Sanctuary	Central Mindanao	Freshwater marsh
Tubbataha Reef Marine National Park	Palawan	Coral reefs and atolls
Apo Reef Marine Natural Park	Mindoro	Coral reefs and atolls
Turtle Islands Marine Turtle Sanctuary	Tawi-Tawi	Coral islands

otter and **mouse deer**. Philippine endemic species include the **tamaraw**, a wild buffalo that survives only on Mindoro, as well as several species of deer. Apart from this, most of the mammals are rather small, consisting largely of **bats** and **rodents**.

The Philippines' most famous bird is undoubtedly the **Philippine eagle**, the world's second-largest raptor. It lives in the rain forests, but loss of habitat has brought it close to extinction. It survives in Mindanao and Luzon, and possibly Samar and Leyte.

Conservation

Although the country had one of the world's first national park systems, set up during the American colonial period, since independence the rapid population growth and lack of concern for the environment have led to devastation. Since World War II, for example, 90 per cent of lowland forests have been lost, with only those in the mountains surviving. At sea, areas of coral reefs have been ruined by dynamite and cyanide fishing. As a result many species are endangered, soil erosion has become severe, water supplies are at risk, and fisheries have been decimated.

Since the early 1990s a major international programme has been started to increase conservation. Dynamite fishing has been stopped in many areas, and reefs are now starting to recover. On land, a new protected areas system has been launched, with 10 of the most important surviving wild areas gaining close protection, along with improved funding and management for many of the pre-existing national parks. Projects that attempt to make sustainable use of the natural environment are mushrooming, including projects centred around ecotourism. There is still quite a long way to go, however, and long-term success still hangs in the balance.

SHRINKING FORESTS

It is estimated that originally 94 per cent of the country was forested, and as recently as 1946 much of the country remained covered with forest. Since then, however, deforestation has been rapid, and now only about 8 per cent natural forest cover remains. This has been due to a combination of logging and slash-and-burn farming, the latter known in the Philippines as **kaingin**. While logging has been banned, it continues on a small scale in some areas. *Kaingin*, however, is still a major activity – the result of rapid population growth and rural poverty. Attempts to protect the remaining forests are partly focusing on ways to find alternative, sustainable livelihoods for the rural poor.

Below: *At barely 8cm (3 inches) the Philippine tarsier is one of the world's smallest primates.*

Below: *An exhibit of a Hagabi (clan bench) as used by the Ifugao people, Northern Luzon.*

HISTORY IN BRIEF
Prehistory

The earliest signs of human life go back 750,000 years, to finds made in the Cagayan Valley in the far north. It is likely, however, that these were formed by *Homo erectus*, the predecessor of *Homo sapiens*. The first signs of the latter date to 30,000–50,000 years ago, mainly from the **Tabon Caves** in Palawan. It is believed that they were related to today's **Negritos**, a tribal group that continues to live in the forests and mountains of some parts of the country.

About 5000 years ago the islands received a wave of immigration: **Austronesian** peoples, probably travelling from their homeland in southern China and/or Taiwan. They occupied the whole country and then fanned out, travelling east and west to populate Southeast Asia and much of the Pacific. Later there were more, smaller immigrations, mostly **Malays** coming in from Borneo.

The Early Philippines

No central power arose to make the Philippines a single country. Instead, the people lived in autonomous clusters of villages, or *barangays*, each with its own chieftain. In time, some places became important trading centres, often outposts of the Indianized empires of Southeast Asia. These places became part of the developing Asian maritime trade routes very early on.

By the 10th century, Filipino merchants were sailing to China for business; ships from China's Song and Yuan dynasties (AD 960–1368) traded extensively with the Philippines. Large finds of Chinese pottery and coins indicate that the main Philippine trading centres were at **Butuan** (on the north coast of Mindanao), **Cebu**, **Tondo** (a district in today's Manila) and the **Sulu Islands**.

From the 13th century, **Arab missionaries** began arriving in the Sulu Islands on Chinese ships, starting the Islamization of the southwest. Sulu's first Islamic sultanate was established in 1450 under **Sayyid Abu Bakr**, a refugee prince from Sumatra. Islam then spread northwards into Mindanao.

At this time **Tondo**, on the northern shore of the Pasig River roughly in the area of today's Binondo district of Manila, came under the control of the Brunei empire. Many Malays and Chinese settled here, forming the nucleus of modern Manila's Chinatown. Brunei also established a settlement on the southern shore of the Pasig, right at the river's mouth, which was possibly called **Maynilad**, the predecessor of today's Manila.

Above: *Raha Humabon, chief of Cebu, is christened by Magellan, in the Philippines' first baptism.*

The Arrival of the Spanish

Ferdinand Magellan, a Portuguese working in the service of Spain, left Spain in 1519, intent on finding a route to the Spice Islands. On 16 March 1521 he and his men arrived off the coast of Samar. Their first landfall was on **Homonhon**, an island just south of Samar. From here they sailed to **Limasawa**, and then to Cebu, where they arrived on 7 April 1521. The chief of Cebu, **Raha Humabon**, was remarkably friendly, and within days Magellan had baptized him and many of his followers.

Magellan then made a fatal error. Humabon's neighbour, **Lapu-Lapu**, chief of nearby **Mactan Island**, was causing trouble, and Magellan decided to settle matters with a fight. Things went wrong, and on **27 April 1521** Magellan was killed by Lapu-Lapu. Many of Magellan's officers were massacred by Humabon's men, the survivors fleeing aboard their ships. Over a year later, they returned to Spain, only 18 men out of the original 265.

FERDINAND MAGELLAN

A Portuguese adventurer, Magellan took part in the battle that captured the Malay port of Malacca for Portugal in 1511. He believed he could reach the Spice Islands of Indonesia from Europe by sailing westwards, but could not convince the Portuguese king to sponsor a test voyage. In 1518, he had more success with the Spanish king, and in 1519 set out with five ships from the Spanish port of San Lucar. Although he was killed in the Philippines and few of the crew survived, the voyage was a historic triumph. This was the first circumnavigation of the globe, proving the Earth to be round and that one could indeed reach the Spice Islands by sailing west.

Above: *A statue of Miguel Lopez de Legaspi.*
Opposite: *Intramuros – the Philippines' walled city.*

Between 1523 and 1546 Spain sent three more expeditions, and by the 1550s the islands had become known as **Islas Filipinas**, in honour of King Philip II of Spain. But not until 1565 and an expedition led by **Miguel de Legaspi** did Spain start to gain a hold on the Philippines. In that year Legaspi set up the first permanent Spanish settlement in Cebu, though fears of an attack by the Portuguese led him to move to Panay.

In the following year, the Spanish decided to attack Manila. An invasion force arrived in May 1570, and after some initial friendly contact a fight started, as a result of which Manila burned. Despite their victory, the Spanish withdrew to Panay. They returned in May 1571, and this time the Malay leaders surrendered. The Spanish city of Manila was born. From being a simple wooden settlement, attacks by the Chinese pirate **Li Mahong** and repeated fires led to its development as a highly fortified stone city, very similar to the **Intramuros** that we see today.

HISTORICAL CALENDAR

circa 60,000–20,000BC Man inhabits Tabon Caves, Palawan.
c1BC Rice terraces of Banaue constructed.
c AD960 Chinese goods begin to appear in the Philippines.
c1100 Chinese colonies are founded along the coasts.
c1200 Islam starts to filter into the far south of the Philippines.
1521 Ferdinand Magellan arrives in the Philippines.
1565 Miguel Lopez de Legaspi arrives in Cebu and sets up first permanent Spanish settlement.
1571 Legaspi takes possession of Manila and makes it the capital of the Philippines.
1600–1617 The Dutch try unsuccessfully to take the Philippines.
1762–4 The British occupy Manila.
1834 Manila is opened to world trade.

1861 Birth of José Rizal.
1887 José Rizal's novel, *Noli me Tangere*, is published in Berlin.
1892 Andres Bonifacio founds the Katipunan, dedicated to ending Spanish rule.
1896, August Bonifacio launches the Philippine Revolution.
1896, December José Rizal is executed.
1898, April The US Congress declares war on Spain.
1898, 12 June The Philippines declares independence.
1898, August Spain surrenders Manila to the USA.
1898, December In the Treaty of Paris, the USA buys the Philippines from Spain.
1899 The Philippine–American War breaks out.
1902 Resistance to American rule ends.

1935 The Commonwealth of the Philippines is inaugurated.
1941 Japan attacks.
1942 US–Filipino forces surrender to the Japanese.
1944 General Douglas MacArthur leads the American landings on Leyte.
1945 Japanese occupaton ends.
1946, 4 July The country gains independence.
1972 President Marcos declares martial law.
1983 Opposition leader Benigno Aquino is assassinated.
1986, 7 Feb A snap election sees Marcos 're-elected'.
1986, 25 Feb The People's Power Revolution deposes Marcos. Corazon Aquino becomes president.
1998, 12 June Centennial celebrations for the country's declaration of independence.

Spanish Rule

The Spanish extended their influence throughout lowland Luzon and the Visayas. Catholic priests were able to convert the Filipinos in their tens of thousands, greatly easing the spread of Spanish control. To govern the population the many scattered settlements were compressed into towns and villages built around a church. The Spanish religious authorities also took it upon themselves to destroy everything they could of the pre-Hispanic era. They did a very thorough job, wiping out records of life before their arrival and completely doing away with the native alphabet – a script similar in appearance to other non-Roman alphabets still in use in parts of South and Southeast Asia today.

With regard to trade, one of the most famous developments was the **Manila Galleons**, the annual sailing of a ship from Manila to Acapulco in Mexico, loaded up with trade goods and treasure. The annual event began early in the city's life and continued until 1815, making a few people immensely rich, though it was of no benefit to the country as a whole. Ironically, the success of trade between Manila and other parts of East Asia depended on the **Chinese community**. They became an essential part of the economy, but the Spanish always mistrusted them. As a result, the Chinese were never allowed into Intramuros and they were forced to live on the banks of the Pasig River, within range of the walled city's guns.

THE MANILA GALLEONS (1565–1815)

For 250 years the Spanish of the Philippines ran the only regular shipping service across the Pacific. Each year two galleons, one each heading east and west, travelled between Manila and Acapulco. The ship leaving Manila would carry trade goods from the Philippines, Southeast Asia and China, paid for by the returning ship in Mexican silver dollars. The round trip took about 200 days. The trade made fortunes for a small number of Manila Spaniards, but went into decline in the late 18th century following the foundation of the Royal Philippine Company, which shipped goods directly to Spain via the Cape of Good Hope.

THE *ENCOMIENDA* SYSTEM

Set up in the earliest days of Spanish rule, this was the awarding of parcels of land, including all the people on it, to men who had served the Spanish crown. The owner of an *encomienda* could exact taxes and loyalty from the people on 'his' land, and had to give protection in return. However, this was usually abused, leading to exploitation of the local people. It was the start of absentee landlordism, with the establishment of huge estates and the concentration of land, and hence power, into a few hands. Such land ownership patterns continue today, despite government's claims to be supporting land reform.

JOSÉ RIZAL (1861–96)

Seen today as the founding father of the nation, his statue can be seen in the centre of almost every town and city. Born in Calamba close to the southern shore of Laguna de Bay, he studied medicine, initially in Manila and later in Madrid. He studied further in London, Heidelberg, Paris and Berlin, returning to the Philippines in 1892. While in Europe he wrote extensively about Spanish oppression in the Philippines, including his two books *Noli me Tangere* and *El Filibusterismo*. Back in the Philippines he founded a pro-democracy movement, Liga Filipina, and was quickly exiled to Mindanao. When the revolution broke out in 1896 he was brought back to Manila for trial, and was executed on 30 December 1896.

Rebellion and the Independence Movement

From the earliest days of Spain's occupation, rebellions were common. The most famous of the early uprisings were those in the far north, led by husband and wife **Diego** and **Gabriela Silang**, but a more truly successful rebellion occurred on Bohol. In 1744 **Francisco Dagohoy** succeeded in wresting independence for the island, something which lasted until 1829 when the Spanish finally succeeded in re-invading.

During the 19th century European liberal ideas of democracy spread to the Philippines via Filipinos who had studied in Europe. These men campaigned for democracy at home, one of the foremost of whom was **José Rizal** (1861–96). His two novels *Noli me Tangere* (meaning 'Don't Touch Me') and *El Filibusterismo* (meaning 'Subversion') exposed the corruption of the Spanish Philippine government and predicted a revolution. His books were banned in the Philippines, and after returning home he was exiled to Mindanao.

While Rizal favoured peaceful change, others were for open rebellion. One, **Andres Bonifacio**, formed the

Katipunan in 1892, an organization dedicated to the violent overthrow of the Spanish. Its membership grew by tens of thousands, and when its secret network was discovered in 1896 Bonifacio launched the revolution. The colonial government accused Rizal of involvement and executed him on the edge of what is now Rizal Park, just outside Intramuros, on 30 December 1896. The **Philippine Revolution** had its greatest martyr.

Fighting went on for several months, during which time an internal struggle broke out within the Katipunan, resulting in the execution of Bonifacio, and the emergence of a new leader, **Emilio Aguinaldo**. The Spanish were unable to put the revolution down, but neither could the Filipinos defeat the Spanish.

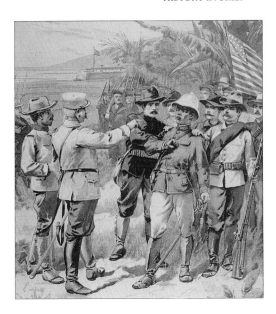

Left: *The capture of General Emilio Aguinaldo, first president of the Philippine Republic, by American troops brought to an end resistance to American rule.*
Opposite: *A statue of Gabriela Silang, first heroine of the Philippine independence movement, stands before the Stock Exchange Tower in Makati.*

At the end of 1897 a truce was finally agreed, with the leaders of the revolution going into exile in Hong Kong.

Peace did not last long, however, due in part to the outbreak of the **Spanish–American War**, resulting from a dispute over Cuba. The USA made plans to invade the Philippines and encouraged the exiles to return home. In May 1898, combined American and Filipino forces laid siege to Manila, and on **12 June 1898** the new Philippine government declared independence from Spain. Freedom was short-lived. The Spanish agreed to surrender, but only to the Americans and only with a face-saving mock battle that excluded the Filipino forces. In this way the Americans took Manila on 13 August 1898, with Aguinaldo and his men frozen out.

Any doubts over the USA's intentions were dispelled by the **Treaty of Paris**, signed in December 1898, in which the USA bought the Philippines from Spain for US$20 million. The Filipinos were soon at war with their new masters, but it was a one-sided fight that ended in Aguinaldo's capture.

HEROES OF THE REVOLUTION

There is a long roll call of people who played a major part in the Philippine Revolution against Spanish rule. Some of the main individuals were as follows:
Apolinario Mabini: the brains of the revolution who drafted the first constitution.
Emilio Aguinaldo: a leading general in the revolution, who became the first president of the new republic, declared on 12 June 1898.
José Rizal: an intellectual whose writings stirred the country towards independence. He was executed by the Spanish.
Andres Bonifacio: a leading general who set up the Katipunan in 1892 and launched the revolution in 1896.
Antonio Luna: a leading general, murdered by his own men.
Emilio Jacinto: founder of the Katipunan and a leading commander.

Above: *Ruins litter Corregidor, the island fortress guarding the entrance to Manila Bay. They stand as silent testament to the battles that have raged around it in the past.*

THE HUKBALAHAP

During the Japanese occupation there was a very active resistance movement. Several guerrilla groups were able to control large territories, running them on socialist lines and bringing about extensive land reform. The largest of these groups was the Hukbalahap, a communist organization which controlled parts of northern and central Luzon. With liberation in 1945, the Huk were reluctant to give up their territory and the land reform they had achieved, and so were outlawed and repressed. They returned to guerrilla activities and were not finally defeated until the mid-1950s.

American Colonial Rule

The early years of the USA's occupation were marked by the occasional brutal suppression of an uprising, but overall the government grew relatively benign. The elite of Philippine society were easily persuaded to cooperate and by the 1910s a US-style congress was established that was largely controlled by wealthy Filipinos, though its powers could be vetoed by the American governor.

The possibility of total independence was raised as early as 1916, but a change in US policy in the early 1920s led to an indefinite delay in the process. However, by early 1933 it had been agreed that the Philippines would pass through a commonwealth phase, starting in 1935 and culminating in full independence on 4 July 1946. On 8 February 1935 the Commonwealth of the Philippines was inaugurated with **Manuel Quezon** as president.

World War II

Preparations for full independence were smashed in December 1941 when the Japanese bombed Pearl Harbor. Within hours American bases in the Philippines were bombed and before year's end, Manila. In December Japanese forces landed in many places in the Philippines. The outnumbered American forces, along with members of the Philippine government, retreated to **Corregidor Island** and the **Bataan Peninsula** in the mouth of Manila Bay. The Japanese entered Manila on 2 January 1942.

The besieged US–Filipino force held out for several months, though once Manuel Quezon and the US commander, **Douglas MacArthur**, had been ordered to leave, resistance weakened. Bataan surrendered in April 1942, followed by Corregidor in May.

There followed three years of Japanese rule, characterized by continual guerrilla warfare against the occupiers; but by 1944 the Americans were returning. On **20 October 1944**, US forces under MacArthur landed on **Red Beach** on the east coast of Leyte. Further landings on Mindoro in December and then in the Lingayen Gulf north of Manila in January 1945 brought the USA to within striking distance of the capital. After heavy fighting Manila fell on 3 February 1945.

Independence

Despite the war the country received full independence on 4 July 1946, as planned. The first president of the new republic was **Manuel Roxas**.

Since then, the Philippines has maintained its US-inspired democracy, one closely allied with the USA. The country became a major bastion in the West's fight against the spread of Communism, numerous American bases being maintained across the country. The most important were the naval base at **Subic Bay** and the nearby **Clark Airforce Base**, both of which saw extensive service during the Vietnam War. The presence of the US military became a sovereignty issue, and when the 1991 eruption of **Mt Pinatubo** caused massive damage to Subic and Clark it became relatively simple for the Philippine Congress to ask the Americans to leave. The US pulled out in 1992.

For most of the postwar period the Philippines has remained democratic. One major hiccup, however, was the Marcos dictatorship. **Ferdinand Marcos** was elected president in 1965 on a wave of optimism that he would provide a fairer distribution of the country's wealth. He was popular for the first few years, but when he declared martial

---

HEY, JOE!

Most visitors will hear this cry as they walk along the streets. To many Filipinos every Westerner is called Joe, a leftover from the American 'GI Joe' days, and apparently they believe it appropriate to yell 'Hey, Joe!' across the street at you. This phenomenon is especially prevalent in areas where foreigners are uncommon, and is something that is simply to be tolerated. In a few areas, such as Camiguin Island, the call has been modernized to the far nicer 'Hello, friend!'

Below: *At the village of Bacolor, near San Fernando, Pampanga province, houses buried up to their eaves in ash bear witness to the immensity of the lahar flows that poured down the slopes of Mt Pinatubo in the wake of its June 1991 eruption.*

THE NEW PEOPLE'S ARMY

The concentration of land ownership into a few hands has provided fertile ground for communist groups. The most powerful of these is the New People's Army, which was formed in 1967 and rose to a peak of activity in the late 1980s. At that time it consisted of 26,000 men and controlled rural areas right across the country. In the mid-1990s President Fidel Ramos made a peace deal with the NPA, which included faster land reform, and since then there has been little guerrilla activity. The NPA still exists, however, and could become popular again if the government fails to deliver on land reform.

Below: *The annual Independence Day celebrations, held on 12th June in Manila, are a reminder of the country's long struggle for self-determination.*

law in 1972 it served only to maintain his grip on power. The next few years were marked by oppression, corruption and a massive siphoning off of the country's wealth.

By the early 1980s the country was nearly bankrupt, and when **Benigno Aquino**, a popular opposition politician, was assassinated in 1983, literally as he was stepping off an airplane at Manila Airport upon his return from exile, the end was near for Marcos. An election in February 1986 saw all the opposition parties give their support to Aquino's widow **Corazon Aquino** in a joint move to push Marcos out. The vote clearly went in favour of Aquino, but Marcos claimed victory and held onto power.

A military coup followed but failed, and as army units loyal to Marcos moved to attack the rebels, the Archbishop of Manila, **Cardinal Jaime Sin**, called on all the people of Manila to come to their protection. Hundreds of thousands of people turned out, blocking the path of the government forces and daring them to open fire on unarmed civilians. The US flew Marcos out to exile, and the **People's Power Revolution** triumphed. Corazon Aquino became the next president.

A new constitution was written and the country gradually put back on its feet. But Aquino was not a skilled leader. She failed to tackle many of the underlying causes of poverty and was unable to stimulate the economy. Discontent soared, leading to numerous insurrections. By the late 1980s the communist **New People's Army** (NPA) controlled large parts of the countryside, especially on Mindanao. On this island too, Islamic separatists, mainly the **Moro National Liberation Front** (MNLF), controlled large areas.

In 1992 an election gave the presidency to **Fidel Ramos**. He made peace deals with the NPA and MNLF, quickly moved to improve the atmosphere for foreign investment, and set in motion a programme, called **Philippines 2000**, to industrialize the country and boost levels of education and training by the end of the century. By the late 1990s the economy was turning around, going from one of the worst in Asia to one of its most rapidly growing. Nevertheless, poverty is still widespread today, and although the NPA's activity is at a low ebb, frustration at the slow pace of land reform is simmering. It remains to be seen whether the president elected in May 1998, **Joseph Estrada**, will be able to deliver a better deal for the country's poor.

Above: *The Philippine flag, decorated with three stars arranged in an equilateral triangle and a shining sun at its centre, is a combination of various symbols used by the Katipunan during the Philippine Revolution.*

GOVERNMENT AND ECONOMY
Government and Politics

Since independence the Philippines has been a **republic** with a national government modelled on American lines, including a powerful elected **President** and a bicameral **Congress**. Congress's upper house, the **Senate**, consists of 24 senators, while the lower house, the **House of Representatives**, has 200 members. The president is elected every six years, and since the Marcos era has been allowed only one term of office. The senators are also elected every six years, half of the 24 standing in a national election every three years.

Members of the House of Representatives are elected every three years, each candidate standing as a regional representative and eligible to sit for up to three terms. The number of representatives each region is allowed to send to Congress depends on the local population.

There are a number of political parties, the principal ones being the Democratic Filipino Struggle **(LDP)**, People Power – National Union of Christian Democrats (NUCD or **Lakas**) and the Nationalist People's Coalition **(NPC)**. However, personalities seem to be more important than parties or their policies.

ECONOMIC INDICATORS

Gross Domestic Product (GDP) • US$256 billion
Gross Domestic Product (GDP) growth • 1.7 per cent
Per capita Gross National Product (GNP) • US$1203
Annual inflation rate • 10.6 per cent
Exports Aug 97–Aug 98 • US$27.4 billion
Current account balance • US$3.8 billion
Reserves (excluding gold) • US$8.6 billion

DEMOGRAPHICS

Total population • 72.6 million
Population annual growth rate • 2.3 %
Life expectancy • 67
Birth rate • 30.42 per 1000 population
Death rate • 6.97 per 1000 population
Infant mortality rate • 49.6 per 1000 live births
Fertility rate • 3.81 children born per woman
Literacy rate • 94 %
Urban population • 46 %

Above: *The houses of workers at a seaweed farm stand in the shallows over Arena Reef.*

LOCAL GOVERNMENT

Below national government are three tiers of local government: provincial, municipal and *barangay*. The elected officials of the provincial government consist of the provincial governor and board members, the latter the province's elected assembly. Each province is divided into municipalities, each with an elected mayor and an elected assembly known as the *sanguniang*. Each municipality is divided into *barangays* – rural villages or urban districts – governed by an elected *barangay* captain and council. The *barangay* officials are elected every five years; the provincial and municipal representatives every three.

Unlike the USA, the Philippines is not a federal nation. The country is divided into 15 major **regions** and below that into 77 **provinces**. Each province is further divided into **municipalities**, centred on a major town or city. Below the municipal level comes the *barangay*, which in the countryside usually equates to a single village, but which in an urban setting is usually one district or ward of a town or city. All members of local government are elected.

Economy

Since the mid-1990s the economy has been recovering rapidly from the devastation caused by the Marcos years. Annual growth rates have been recorded at 5–6 per cent, and even with the Asian financial crisis, which started in 1997, the economy has continued to grow despite a 30–40 per cent drop in the value of the local currency, the **Peso**.

Although **industry** has developed over the past few years – centred mainly around Manila and Cebu City and producing processed foods, clothing and electrical goods – the country depends mostly on the primary products of agriculture and mining. The Philippines is Southeast Asia's biggest producer of **copper** and is in the top ten worldwide, with the world's largest copper mine in Cebu. **Gold** and **silver** are also abundant, Benguet province in the Cordillera Central being the main producer. Another important mineral is **chromite**, while zinc, manganese, iron ore and cobalt are also present in small quantities. The search for oil beneath Philippine waters has so far had only limited success.

Despite the steadily growing industrial sector, **agriculture** is still the country's main employer. The principal agricultural products are rice, corn (maize), sugar cane, pineapples, coconuts (including copra) and bananas. A number of these crops are produced on small family-owned holdings, but most of them come from large estates.

Remittances sent from the many Filipinos working overseas are also an important factor in the economy. Although the cost of living is low, **poverty** is still widespread, with incomes in rural areas as low as US$40 per month. One of the problems that has persisted since the Spanish era is the unequal distribution of land, with **huge estates** concentrated into a few hands, leaving a large number of people with no secure tenure anywhere. The government's long-term failure to tackle this inequality is one of the major causes of the discontent and communist rebellions that have simmered since independence.

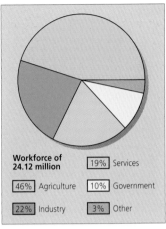

Workforce of 24.12 million

- 19% Services
- 46% Agriculture
- 10% Government
- 22% Industry
- 3% Other

Below: *An open cast gold mine in Mindanao.*

UBIQUITOUS RICE

Rice is the main staple for almost all Filipinos, each person eating about 100kg (220 lb) per year, accounting for about 35 per cent of their calorie intake. The crop accounts for over 20 per cent of the total agricultural output, and is grown on 3.2 million ha (8 million acres) of land, half of it irrigated. Its value is estimated at US$275 million. However, the country's rapidly growing population ensures that in most years rice has to be imported. The International Rice Research Institute (IRRI), near Los Banos, is in a constant race to find ways to improve productivity to keep up with growing needs.

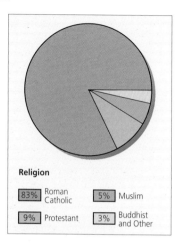

Religion

| 83% | Roman Catholic | 5% | Muslim |
| 9% | Protestant | 3% | Buddhist and Other |

THE PEOPLE

The Filipinos of today are a curious blend of East and West, showing strong Malay, Chinese, Spanish and American inputs. While the first has laid the basic groundwork in terms of the people's physical appearance, temperament and main language structure, influences from the other three have been absorbed: nothing foreign has been rejected, but taken in and adapted to local use.

The vast majority of today's Filipinos are descended from Austronesians who migrated from the north 5000 years ago, founding the Philippine, Malay and Polynesian peoples as they travelled and colonized. In many areas there is an overlay of more recent Malay immigrations, particularly in and around Panay.

A Spanish legacy takes the form of numerous phrases and words absorbed into the vernacular, most importantly in names of places and people. It is a similar story with the American influence, which has led Christian names, for example, to be pronounced in the anglicized manner even if given a Spanish spelling. Many aspects of urban lifestyle are also remnants of the American past, including a yearning for the 'American Dream'. There are still extensive family and business connections between the Philippines and the USA.

PHILIPPINE ENGLISH

While it is true to say that English is widely spoken across the Philippines, it is often used in ways that may not be familiar to visiting native speakers. For one thing, to many Filipinos the spoken vocabulary is often closer than normal to the written language, sometimes making their speech seem rather stiff and overly formal, something quite incongruous in an otherwise generally informal people.

Right: *A brightly painted tricycle takes a school girl to class; Dumaguete, Negros Oriental.*
Opposite: *A young fishing family sift through their nets for fish after a trawl along the sea shore; Siargao Island, Mindanao.*

Another major American legacy is the widespread use of English. One of the country's two official languages, its teaching is compulsory in school and it is often the principal language in business and government. This tends to create a barrier to advancement for the poorer, less educated parts of society. Nevertheless, the visitor will find that even the poorest fisherman is able to make basic English conversation.

Few people, however, use English as their first language. There are said to be over 80 languages and dialects in the Philippines, though the vast majority speak one or more of the eight principal tongues: Tagalog, Ilocano, Pangasinan, Pampangan, Bicol, Cebuano, Waray-Waray and Ilongo (also called Hiligaynon). With 30 per cent of the population speaking **Tagalog**, including those in the Manila area, this has become, in a standardized form called **Pilipino**, the other official national language.

Daily Life

One of the most striking features of Philippine life is the prominence of women. While raising a family is a major goal for the great majority of Filipinos and Filipinas, as men and women are respectively called, this does not prevent women achieving senior positions and success in government and business. That this is possible is partly due to the strength of the extended family, young women being freed to work by grandparents who can look after children. It is also due to the inequality in society that enables wealthier people to employ those from the poorer levels of society as house- and childminders on low wages.

The strength of the extended family is important in allowing poor families, especially in the countryside, collectively to make a living. In wealthier families strong ties of kinship make it possible for family members to help each other succeed.

THE JEEPNEY

The jeepney is the ubiquitous form of public transport, unique to the Philippines. It was born at the end of World War II out of a desperate shortage of public transport vehicles and an excess of US military jeeps. Workshops sprang up to lengthen the jeeps' chassis, fit benches down the sides and put a roof over the top. Today they still dominate the roads, though they have come some way since 1945, and not just the padding on the benches. Painted and decorated with flamboyant designs, slogans and even statuettes, many are mobile works of pop art. Most are also equipped with very powerful hi-fi systems, used to considerable effect, and a few are even decorated with flashing lights.

Above: *On Good Friday penitents allow themselves to be nailed to a cross.*
Below: *Life in an Ifugao village, Cordillera Central.*

The problem of finding sufficient work in the Philippines has led many to work overseas. Filipinas are frequently seen in domestic work in Hong Kong and other wealthy Asian countries, while men are common in the oil industry of the Middle East and the world's merchant shipping. Their remittances are an important contribution to maintaining families back home.

The need to generate as many workers as possible in a poor family, along with a genuine love of children and a Roman Catholic opposition to birth control, has created a rapidly growing population. Already standing at 72 million, the population's annual growth rate is about 2.3 per cent, one of the highest in Asia, and shows little sign of slowing down. To date, only the educated classes have recognized the need to limit family size.

Religion plays a central part in daily life. Ninety per cent of the population is Christian, 5 per cent Muslim and the remainder a mixture of Buddhist and animist. Of the Christians 92 per cent are Roman Catholic, 8 per cent Protestant. There are a couple of home-grown Christian groups, notably Iglesia ni Cristo, a nationalistic protestant group, and the Philippine Independent Church, a Catholic body. Attendance of mass and personal prayer are common, often combined with some folk superstitions, a remnant of pre-Christian days.

Ethnic and Tribal Groups

About 10 per cent of the population belongs to one of the country's many ethnic minorities, about half of these **Muslims** in the far south. Of the remainder, an important element are the **Negritos**, often called by a variety of names, such as Aeta or Agta. Now numbering less than 15,000 they are mainly scattered across Panay and Luzon. They prefer to live in remote forests and mountains, and are all that remains of the country's first inhabitants.

Other important groups, most of them numerically stronger than the Negritos, include the Ifugao, Bontoc, Kalinga, Mangyan, T'boli, Manobo, Tausug, Badjao and Tagbanua. The first three live in the Cordillera Central of northern Luzon. Warlike people that used to be headhunters, they have traditionally been resistant to outside control and were only integrated into the Philippines during American rule. It was the **Ifugao** who 2000 years ago built the stupendous rice terraces on the hills around Banaue. The **Mangyan** are the main inhabitants of Mindoro, living mostly in the interior. A large group, they are subdivided, those in the north and the south speaking mutually incomprehensible languages. The **Manobo** live scattered across eastern Mindanao and the **T'boli** live in the southwestern part of this island, while the **Tausug** are the main Muslim inhabitants of the Sulu Islands. The **Badjao** live on the Sulu Islands and Palawan, on boats or in houses built on stilts above water. They rarely come onto land, except to be buried. The **Tagbanua** are a rather shy farming group concentrated mostly in northern Palawan.

MAIN TRIBAL OR ETHNIC MINORITIES	
Name	**Location(s)**
Negritos (Aeta, Agta, Ati, Ata, Ita, Dumagat)	Various mountainous regions of Luzon, Panay and Negros
Ilocano	Northern Luzon
Apayao	Northern Luzon
Kalinga	Cordillera Central, in Northern Luzon
Bontoc	Cordillera Central, in Northern Luzon
Ifugao	Cordillera Central, in Northern Luzon
Mangyan (Iraya, Alangan, Tadyawan, Buhid, Hanunoo)	Mindoro
Manobo	Eastern and Central Mindanao
Bagobo	Southern Mindanao
Tasaday	Southern Mindanao
T'boli	Southern Mindanao
Mandaya	Southern Mindanao
Maranao	Western Mindanao
Samal	Western Mindanao
Subanon	Western Mindanao
Yakan	Western Mindanao and Basilan Island
Tausug	Sulu Islands
Badjao	Sulu Islands and Palawan
Tagbanua	Palawan (especially Calamian Islands)
Batak	Palawan
Tau't Batu	Palawan
Pala'wan	Palawan
Jama Mapun	Southern Palawan

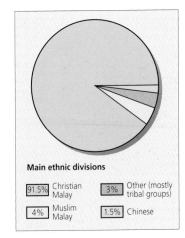

Main ethnic divisions

91.5% Christian Malay
4% Muslim Malay
3% Other (mostly tribal groups)
1.5% Chinese

Festivals

Festivals are a major part of Philippine life, and always a great spectacle for the visitor. Every city, town and village holds at least one festival every year, usually related to such dates as the 'birthday' of the local patron saint or other religious icon, a harvest thanksgiving for the main local agricultural crop, a historical or mythological anniversary, or a combination of all these. One thing is for sure: this is the annual excuse for the locals to forget their troubles and really let their hair down. Drunkenness, loud music and dancing are essential parts of every festival, though there is usually a more serious religious element, such as a blessing or a special mass. Often there are also parades and competitions, carried out with varying degrees of seriousness. Beauty contests are another popular feature of Philippine life.

Much more serious are the Independence Day parades that occur in Manila on 12 June each year, marking the anniversary of the Declaration of Independence from Spain. A big event, this is mainly a chance for the military to show off its firepower.

Arts and Handicrafts

With its long history of exposure to the West, a large proportion of Philippine art and entertainment is in the European style. This is perhaps most obvious in popular music, where rock, both foreign and home grown, is the

Opposite: *Dancing at Dinagyang Festival, held annually in Iloilo, largest city on Panay.*
Right: *Barbecued chicken and other food stalls on the street during a food festival in Iloilo.*

staple. Filipinos excel as musicians, and there are a large number of bands – producing both their own music and cover versions of famous songs – working as hotel entertainers right across Asia.

However, since independence many Filipino artists have searched for native roots, something made difficult by the long Spanish rule. Slowly, old themes have re-emerged, particularly in the well-established professional **dance** groups, which are an interesting amalgam of Spanish, Malay and tribal. This is most easily seen in the free weekend performances in Intramuros and Rizal Park. Even the orchestras that accompany the dancers reflect the mixed influence, as they switch between Spanish guitars and Malay percussion instruments.

Handicrafts have become a major product, especially among some of the tribal groups, who have found a new livelihood as a result. Produced at least in part for tourism, domestic as well as international, the products are often of high quality and reflect some of the traditional beliefs and skills of the tribal people. **Woodcarvings** of traditional figures are common, along with **basketry** products such as fruit bowls and floor mats. Patterned woven fabics are produced in styles similar to Indonesian **ikats**, while the Muslims of the southwest have colourful dyed fabrics. Interestingly, these handicrafts are slowly appearing in craft shops around the world.

FRUIT

Fruit vendors usually stock apples, oranges and bananas, but there is also a range of tropical fruits:
Durian: A large fruit with a thick, spiny shell, a pungent smell and very sweet taste.
Jackfruit: Similar to durian, but with a smoother, dark green skin. Flesh is yellow.
Kalamansi: A small lime-like fruit, often used in lemon tea.
Lanzones: About the size of a cherry. The skin is peeled off to reveal translucent flesh.
Mango: Usually yellow, with a rich sweet taste.
Mangosteen: Very thick, dark purple skin; pearly white segments with sweet-sour taste.
Rambutan: Egg-shaped with a dry, red, spikey skin and translucent flesh.

2
Metro Manila

Created in the 1970s by the merging of eight cities and nine towns, Metropolitan Manila is the capital of the Philippines – a sprawling city of over 10 million people. For Filipinos in other parts of the country this is El Dorado, constantly drawing them in from the poor countryside. The result is an overcrowded metropolis that is constantly expanding. Traffic congestion and air pollution are problems, and can make Manila rather daunting for the first-time visitor. It is, however, a fascinating place, one that is worth spending time exploring and getting to know.

The section of the city that is **Manila** itself consists of a north–south orientated rectangle on the shore of **Manila Bay**, reaching from the port area north of the **Pasig River** south to the border with Pasay City, in the vicinity of the Philippine International Convention Center. Here are **Chinatown** (where many of the city's Chinese businesses are concentrated), **Intramuros** (the original Spanish city), **Rizal Park** (the green oasis of the inner city) and **Ermita** and **Malate** districts (areas in which many visitors stay).

To the south lie **Pasay** and **Parañaque**, site of the international airport, while to the east is **Makati**, the main business district, home to international companies, chic shopping centres and hotels. This is the modern, wealthy face of Metro Manila. To the northeast is **Quezon City**, centre of the Philippine government. Many of the sightseeing areas are concentrated in the old parts of Manila. For shopping and entertainment, however, head for either Manila's Ermita and Malate, or Makati.

DON'T MISS

** Intramuros: old Spanish walled city, founded 1571, at the mouth of the Pasig River.
** Rizal Park: a green swathe on the southern edge of Intramuros, enjoyable on Sundays.
** Nayong Pilipino: a cultural village showing the various architectural styles found across the Philippines.
* Ayala Museum: a good exhibition of dioramas tracing the history of the Philippines.
* Corregidor Island: a fortified island in the mouth of Manila Bay, fought over by the Spanish, Americans and Japanese.

Opposite: *Traffic crowds Quezon Boulevard, one of Manila's main arteries.*

NORTH OF THE PASIG RIVER

This area is one of the most crowded parts of the city. It consists of numerous narrow shopping streets and jammed **markets**, which are well worth exploring for a taste of Manila life. There are also several **churches**, the massive **Chinese Cemetery** and the **Malacañang Palace**, home to Philippine presidents.

Malacañang Palace *

Situated on the north bank of the Pasig River, this ornate building was originally the home of a Spanish merchant. Early in the 19th century it became the residence of the Spanish and then American heads of government, and when the Philippines gained independence, their own presidents occupied the building. Part of the palace is open to the public as a museum. Open Tues–Wed 09:00–15:30 and Thurs 09:00–12:00 with guided tours; Thurs 13:00–15:00 and Fri–Sat 09:00–15:00 without guided tours.

Quiapo Church and Market *

Situated to the west of the Malacañang Palace is Quiapo Church. Down one side of it runs congested Quezon Boulevard, and to the west is a mass of crowded streets lined with shops and filled with market stalls. This market is always a lively and interesting place to visit. The church itself, on the other hand, is disappointingly modern, having been built only in 1899 and restored in 1935. Its fame stems from what lies inside –

Metro Manila

the statue of the **Black Nazarene**. It is a statue of Jesus bearing a cross, whose wood has weathered in such a way that Jesus has turned almost black. It is said to have been made by an Aztec artist in Mexico, and then brought to Manila at some time in the 17th century. The statue is revered all over the Philippines, and on 9 January each year, on the **Festival of the Black Nazarene**, it is paraded through the streets of Quiapo surrounded by a tumultuous crowd.

Above: *The statue of the Black Nazarene struggles through a seething crowd in Quiapo, during the Festival of the Black Nazarene.*

Chinatown *

This fascinating area stretches more or less from Santa Cruz Church in the east to Binondo Church in the west. Escolta and Ongpin streets are the main shopping thoroughfares. Chinatown has been destroyed several times over the centuries, most recently in 1945. Today, it shows all the signs of having been rather hurriedly and cheaply rebuilt. Dilapidated and terribly overcrowded, it is nevertheless a lively and colourful place to visit, especially in the run-up to Chinese New Year, when the markets are even more crowded than usual.

Chinese Cemetery *

Further to the north is the Chinese Cemetery. This is not the kind of place one would normally recommend for a tour, but it is quite remarkable nonetheless. It is filled with tombs as big as houses, grandiose in both scale and decoration. The tombs are expressions of incredible wealth by their deceased Chinese occupants – some of them are even equipped with electricity and running water, not to mention stained-glass windows. The cemetery is also a peaceful escape from the furore of the city outside.

> **FESTIVAL OF THE BLACK NAZARENE**
>
> The image of Christ as a black man has attracted a large following among the Filipino poor. There are many such images, but the Black Nazarene belonging to Manila's **Quiapo Church** is the most important. Its annual festival is held on 9 January, during which it is pulled through the crowded streets on a hand-drawn carriage. Anyone can take hold of the pulling ropes, and since to touch any part of the statue, including the ropes, is to bring forgiveness for even the worst sins, the statue's exit from the church causes a mass frenzy.

Above: *A view across the walls of Intramuros towards Manila Cathedral.*

SOUTH OF THE RIVER

This is the part of Manila that most visitors to the Philippines come to know well. Here lies the city's main historical landmark, **Intramuros**, and beyond are the districts of **Ermita** and **Malate**, Manila's main tourist area.

Intramuros **

Meaning 'within the walls', this is the old walled city that was the seat of the Spanish colonial adminstration. Today, most of the city is a reconstruction, as much of the original was devastated in 1945.

The walls that surround Intramuros are more or less intact, and it is possible to explore the ramparts in a number of areas. One of the most interesting parts is in the southwest corner, at the **Baluarte de San Diego**, a massive corner bastion built on the site of the

MANILA BEFORE THE SPANISH

A settlement, called Tundun and later Tondo, existed on the north bank of the Pasig River in the 9th century AD – an outpost of Srivijaya, an Indianized Southeast Asian empire. When the empire faded in the 11th century, Tondo gained independence and became heavily involved in trade with the Arabs and Chinese. From early in the 16th century Tondo formed part of the Brunei Empire, at which time another Brunei settlement was established at the mouth of the Pasig River, called **Maynilad**. At the time of the Spanish arrival in 1570, the chief of Tondo was **Raha Lakandula**, and that of Maynilad **Raha Soleiman**, both Muslims. It was these men who fought and then surrendered to the Spanish.

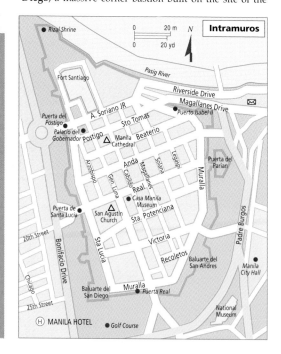

first Spanish fortress. In the southeast corner is another impressive fortification, the **Baluarte de San Andres**.

At the northern end is **Fort Santiago**, guarding the mouth of the Pasig River. Today it forms a pleasant garden and has a memorial to **José Rizal**, the national hero who was imprisoned here before his execution in 1896.

In the centre of Intramuros stands **Manila Cathedral**. The first church was erected here in 1581: the present cathedral is the sixth incarnation, rebuilt in 1958. To the south, on General Luna Street, is **San Agustin Church**, the oldest church in the country, built in 1571. Here is buried **Legaspi**, the Spanish founder of Manila. Miraculously this church has survived fire, earthquake and war. A small museum is attached to the church. Open 09:00–12:00 and 13:00–17:00 daily.

Across the road is the **Plaza San Luis**, a complex of nine reconstructed buildings representing the designs of the different eras of Philippine architecture. Inside is **Casa Manila**, a museum designed to resemble a wealthy 19th-century home. Open 09:00–12:00 and 13:00–18:00 daily.

Rizal Park **

To the south of Intramuros, and separated from it by a golf course, is Rizal Park, popularly known as **Luneta**. This rectangular stretch of green is a popular place for Manila people to relax.

At the western end is **Rizal Monument**, erected close to where the national hero was executed. Behind stretches a **lagoon** with several fountains. To the north are the **Chinese Garden**, **Japanese Garden**, **Planetarium** and **open-air theatre**. The last of these is a good place to watch the free music or dance performances that take place on Sunday afternoons.

At the eastern end of the park is a skating rink, next to the **Department of Tourism**. To the north, on Padre Burgos St, is the **National Museum**, known for its exhibitions on pre-Hispanic Philippines, especially from the prehistoric era. Open Mon–Sat 09:00–12:00 and 13:00–17:00.

SPANISH REMINDERS

Reminders of the Spanish past are scattered around this fast-growing city. The most obvious are the many place names, such as San Juan, San Andres, San Nicolas and Santa Cruz. Solid remains consist mainly of Intramuros, though even much of this is a post-World War II reconstruction. Much of the massive walls, as well as Fort Santiago, are original, as is San Agustin Church, the oldest church in the Philippines. Elsewhere, there is Paco Park, an attractive walled circular park created in the early 1800s. Spanish-era churches include the one at Las Pinas.

Below: *A rainbow spreads across a fountain in the ever popular Rizal Park, known by locals as Luneta.*

Ermita and Malate *

These two districts, running southwards along the shore of Manila Bay, are well-frequented by visitors. Here lie most of the hotels and many services that visitors need, such as travel agencies, money changers and souvenir shops. Although the main thoroughfare, **Roxas Boulevard**, is lined with high-rise buildings, some of them luxury hotels, much of the area is actually rather rundown. A 1990s property boom has gradually started to change this.

At the southern end, the **Zoological and Botanical Garden** is a park that gives an introduction to the country's wildlife, although sadly most of the animals are not kept in good conditions. Open 07:00–18:00 daily.

Further south, on Roxas Boulevard, is the **Metropolitan Museum** (open Tues–Sat 09:00–18:00), a modern building housing rotating exhibitions of foreign and Philippine art. Almost directly opposite, on land reclaimed from the bay, is the **Cultural Center of the Philippines**, which houses not only a large theatre where cultural performances are frequently shown, but also the **Museo ng Kalinangang Pilipino** (open Tues–Sun 10:00–18:00, or 10:00–22:00 when there are evening performances), a beautiful museum housing an exhibition on different aspects of traditional Filipino costume, music and dance. It is well worth a visit.

Left: *A performance of traditional dancing at the Nayong Pilipino cultural village. Such performances are held every Sunday.*
Opposite: *A view of Manila, seen from the Manila Hotel, looking along Roxas Boulevard and the shore of Manila Bay.*

To the east of Ermita, in the district of Paco, is **Paco Park**. This is a pleasant circular walled garden, an oasis in the middle of the city, shaded by some enormous trees.

Nayong Pilipino **

Next to the airport's runways is this interesting cultural village-cum-park. Scattered in its grounds are numerous 'villages' – clusters of houses representing the architecture of different parts of the Philippines. One of the best is Ifugao Village, a cluster of thatched huts from the Cordillera Central of northern Luzon, complete with miniature rice terraces on which rice really is grown.

At one end of a lake are arranged several villages of the southern Philippines, mainly Mindanao and Sulu – groups of houses built in a pleasing architectural style. On Sundays the Mindanao village puts on dance performances. These villages are excellent places to pick up souvenirs of folk handicrafts, each one selling products representative of their part of the country. Close to the Sulu village is the **Museum of Ethnology**, which has an exhibition on the lives of the various ethnic groups of the Philippines.

In another part of the park is a walk-through aviary that contains a collection of Philippine birds. It is rather short on variety, but interesting nonetheless – the trees inside the aviary are so dense it can be quite difficult to see the birds! Open Tues–Sun 09:00–18:00.

PEOPLE'S POWER

One of Asia's most famous modern uprisings took place in Manila in February 1986, following the rigging of presidential elections by then-president Ferdinand Marcos. Marcos claimed that he had defeated his opponent, Corazon Aquino, but when international observers reported the results fraudulent, thousands of people took to the streets. Defence minister **Juan Ponce Enrile** and deputy army chief **General Fidel Ramos** (who later became president) joined the opposition, along with a large section of the army. At separate ceremonies both Marcos and Aquino were sworn in as president. When forces loyal to Marcos moved down one of Manila's main arteries, **EDSA**, to attack the rebels at their base, their way was blocked by hundreds of thousands of people. Marcos was taken into exile by the US military, and ever since then the event has been marked on 25 February by parades along EDSA.

Above: *The massive entrance to the Stock Exchange Tower opens out onto Ayala Avenue.*

MAKATI

Makati is the commercial hub of the capital, if not the entire country, and it is here that many banks and industrial or trading companies have their headquarters. Here you will also find some of the best shopping centres, restaurants and nightclubs, along with the country's smartest hotels.

While most visitors come to Makati for shopping and nightlife, there are also a few opportunities for sightseeing in the area. The first is the **Ayala Museum**, situated on Makati Avenue – an excellent museum that traces the Philippines' history from earliest settlement through to the EDSA Revolution of 1985. It makes use of 63 dioramas, extremely well-made models of events that capture critical moments in the country's history. Open Tues–Sun 09:00–17:30.

On the southeastern side of Makati is **Forbes Park**, an exclusive residential area for the wealthiest Filipinos. Nearby is a golf course, and to the south of that is the **American Cemetery and Memorial**, last resting place for many of the Americans that gave their lives for the Philippines.

INFAMOUS TRAFFIC

Every day the main streets of Manila are clogged with traffic, often virtually immobile for long periods. A journey that at, say, 05:00 takes about 15 minutes, by 07:00 is likely to need at least 45, a situation that does not improve until about 21:00. The government has tried various methods of traffic control, including allowing cars with odd and even numbered plates access to the city only on alternate days, but with little success. The most recent attempt has been improved enforcement of traffic rules, along with a massive increase in fines for offenders, since many problems are caused simply by bad and inconsiderate driving. It remains to be seen whether there will be any improvement.

SHOPPING AND ENTERTAINMENT

For the visitor, shopping and entertainment opportunities are concentrated around Makati and the Ermita/Malate area. The latter has quite a large number of small bars and restaurants, mainly spread out along **Mabini** and **Adriatico** Streets. There are a number of souvenir and handicraft shops in this area. Handicrafts can also be bought in the main department stores, such as Rustans, Robinsons and SM, which, along with many other shops, are concentrated at **Harrison Plaza** (near the zoo) and **Robinsons Mall**, at the northern end of Adriatico Street.

In Makati, the choice of places to visit is huge. Most of the shopping is based around the **Ayala Center**, where you will find the enormous **Glorietta Mall** and also the **Landmark**. Close by is **Greenbelt Square**, where there is another mall, along with several restaurants and a cinema. As with Ermita/Malate, some of the best places to buy handicrafts are the department stores, particularly in the Landmark. The streets around Greenbelt and the Ayala Center are lined with a wide variety of restaurants.

Northeast of Makati, in **Mandaluyong**, a new centre of commerce has sprung up that is starting to rival Makati. Here are several more shopping malls, including the **Shangri-La Plaza** and the enormous **Megamall**.

If you wish to attend cultural performances, these often take place at the **Cultural Center**. Alternatively, there are frequent free performances at the open-air theatre in **Rizal Park**. On Friday and Saturday evenings from January to June, Baluarte de San Diego in **Intramuros** is the venue for free dance performances by highly reputable dance troupes. Contact the Department of Tourism for details.

CORREGIDOR ISLAND

The fortress island of Corregidor lies a 2–3 hour ferry journey to the southwest. Initially fortified by the Spanish, Corregidor was quite heavily fought over by Spanish, American and Japanese invaders, who all recognized its key role in controlling Manila's shipping. Today, the island stands as a memorial to those times, with not only a Spanish lighthouse remaining, but also many of the heavy American fortifications and several memorials to the bloody events. Most visitors come on a day trip, but there is accommodation for those wishing to stay overnight. Ferries leave at 07:30 daily from the wharf close to the Cultural Center.

EIGHT CITIES

Metro Manila comprises eight cities – Manila, Pasay, Makati, Caloocan, Quezon, Pasig, Mandaluyong and Muntinlupa – and is home to 10 million people, making it the largest metropolis in the Philippines.

Below: *A gun emplacement on Corregidor Island serves as a reminder of the grim battles fought here.*

Metro Manila at a Glance

BEST TIMES TO VISIT

Manila's rainy season lasts June–October, when parts of the city are often flooded and getting around can be difficult. The best time is **December** to **March**, when it is sunny, humidity is low and temperatures not too high. April–May can be very hot.

GETTING THERE

Ninoy Aquino International Airport is the Philippines' main international gateway, served by airlines from around the world. All major Asian airlines fly here. The national carrier, Philippine Airlines, also provides direct links with North America. In 1998 it gave up its Australian and European routes, so travellers coming from there may find they will have to fly indirectly.

GETTING AROUND

Manila is highly congested and getting around can be slow. Always allow plenty of time for journeys and do not try to do too much in one day. The **bus** system is a shambles, and **jeepneys**, though plentiful, are crowded, hot and uncomfortable. Recently they have had to face competition from air-conditioned minibuses called **Tamaraws**, and these may improve things. Manila's **taxis** are air-conditioned, very inexpensive and metered only for distance. They are by far the best way to get around town.

If you are travelling north or south in the Ermita/Malate/Chinatown area, the one and only **Light Rail Transit** (LRT) line is excellent. Though often overcrowded, it is a very convenient way of getting around that part of town. Another line which will follow the length of EDSA, circling much of the city, is presently under construction.

WHERE TO STAY

LUXURY
Makati Shangri-La Hotel, Ayala Avenue, corner Makati Avenue, Makati City 1200, Metro Manila, tel: (02) 813-8888, fax: (02) 813-5499. A luxurious hotel right in the centre of Makati, next to the Ayala Center.

EDSA Shangri-La Hotel, 1 Garden Way, Ortigas Center, Mandaluyong City 1650, Metro Manila, tel: (02) 633-8888, fax: (02) 631-1067. A luxurious hotel with a brand new extension, pleasant gardens and large swimming pool, in the new commercial hub of Mandaluyong.

The Manila Hotel, 1 Rizal Park, Manila 1099, tel: (02) 527-0011, fax: (02) 527-0022. The grand old lady of Manila's hotels, opulent and refined. Superb views of Manila Bay.

Holiday Inn, United Nations Avenue, Ermita, Manila 1000, tel: (02) 526-1212, fax: (02) 526-2552. A large, modern hotel on the southern edge of Rizal Park, adjoining Ermita.

Hotel Sofitel Grand Boulevard Manila, 1990 Roxas Boulevard, PO Box 776, Manila 1057, tel: (02) 526-8588, fax: (02) 524-2526. A comfortable hotel in Malate, with nice views of Manila Bay.

MID-RANGE
Traders Hotel Manila, 3001 Roxas Boulevard, Pasay City 1305, Metro Manila, tel: (02) 523-7011, fax: (02) 522-3985. A comfortable and well-run business hotel with views of Manila Bay.

Swagman Hotel Manila, 411 A Flores St, Ermita, Manila, tel: (02) 523-8541, fax: (02) 521-9731. The Philippine headquarters of the Swagman chain, offering value-for-money hotels and travel services over much of the country.

Las Palmas Hotel, 1616 A Mabini St, Malate, Manila, tel: (02) 524-5602, fax: (02) 522-1699. A modern hotel in the Ermita/Malate area.

Royal Palm Hotel, 1227 A Mabini, corner P Faura and Ermita streets, Manila, tel: (02) 522-1515, fax: (02) 522-0768. A value-for-money hotel in the centre of the Ermita/Malate area. Rooms facing the street can be rather noisy; try to get one at the back.

Riviera Mansion, 1638 A Mabini St, Malate, Manila, tel: (02) 521-2381, fax: (02) 522-2606. A good value hotel at the southern end of the Ermita/Malate area.

Metro Manila at a Glance

Makati International Inn, 2178 Pasong Tamo Ave, Makati City, Metro Manila, tel: (02) 892-5989, fax: (02) 819-5722. A friendly hotel on the edge of Makati, complete with its own health spa.

BUDGET

Robelle House, 4402 Valdez St, corner Makati Avenue, Makati City 1210, Metro Manila, tel: (02) 899-8209, fax: (02) 899-8064. An attractive building in the style of a Spanish villa, surrounded by palm trees; an oasis in the city.

Pension Natividad, 1690 MH del Pilar, Malate, Manila 1004, tel: (02) 521-0524, fax: (02) 522-3759. Another oasis, set in its own garden.

WHERE TO EAT

Endangered Species, 1834 MH del Pilar, Malate, Manila, tel: (02) 524-0167, fax: (02) 521-4154. Bar and restaurant, Filipino and Western food.

The Brewery, Level 3, Quad III, Ayala Center, Makati City, Metro Manila, tel: (02) 817-8934, fax: (02) 817-8979. A popular bar selling a range of beers and excellent bar meals.

Zen Restaurant, Level 1, Quad III, Ayala Center, Makati City, Metro Manila, tel: (02) 892-6851. A popular Japanese restaurant near The Brewery.

Islands Fisherman Seafood Restaurant, Arquiza St, Ermita, Manila, tel: (02) 521-9490. An excellent seafood restaurant.

Studebaker's Makati, Glorietta 3, Ayala Center, Makati City, Metro Manila, tel: (02) 893-1841. American food, live music and disco.

La Tasca Restaurant, Legaspi St, Makati City, Manila, tel: (02) 819-5435. A popular and pleasantly decorated Italian restaurant.

TOURS AND EXCURSIONS

For the trip to Corregidor Island contact **Sun Cruises**. For trips to many other areas **Swagman Travel** can make arrangements. There are a number of car-hire companies offering both self-drive and chauffeur-driven hire cars. To arrange any diving trips before leaving Manila, contact **Whitetip Divers**: this company specializes in putting together complete diving packages, including your domestic flight arrangements.

USEFUL CONTACTS

Department of Tourism, Department of Tourism Building, TM Kalaw St, Ermita, Manila, tel: (02) 524-2345, fax: (02) 524-8321, e-mail: dotncr@mnl.sequel.net.

Assistance line, tel: (02) 524-1703.

Philippine Airlines, PAL Building, Legaspi St, Makati City, Metro Manila, tel: (02) 817-1479 (international), (02) 817-1509 (domestic). S&L Building, 1500 Roxas Boulevard, Ermita, Manila, tel: (02) 521-8821 or use the 24-hour line: 816-6691-5.

Swagman Travel, 411 A Flores St, Ermita, Manila, tel: (02) 523-8541, fax: (02) 522-3663, e-mail: bookings@swaggy.com.

Safari Rent-a-Car, 1942 Flordeliz St, La Paz Village, Makati City, Metro Manila, tel: (02) 890-3606, fax: (02) 899-2304.

Nissan Car Lease Philippines, UPRC III Building, 2289 Pasong Tamo Extension, Makati City, Metro Manila, tel: (02) 810-6845.

Whitetip Divers, Joncor II Building, Unit 206/9, 1362 A Mabini St, Ermita, Manila, tel: (02) 526-8190, fax: (02) 522-1165, e-mail: whitetip@info.com.ph.

Police, Western District, tel: 166 or (02) 523-8391. Makati, tel: (02) 899-9008.

MANILA	J	F	M	A	M	J	J	A	S	O	N	D
AVERAGE TEMP. °F	79	81	82	84	86	84	82	82	82	82	81	81
AVERAGE TEMP. °C	26	27	28	29	30	29	28	28	28	28	27	27
RAINFALL ins.	0.6	0.2	0.4	0.7	5.7	11.2	16	18.3	13.9	8.8	4.8	2
RAINFALL mm	16	6	9	17	146	284	408	464	352	224	122	52
DAYS OF RAINFALL	4	2	2	3	9	17	22	22	20	17	11	7

3
Northern Luzon and Batanes Islands

Encompassing the main body of Luzon, the largest of the Philippines' islands, this area covers all the land north of Manila. Much of the landscape here is quite different from the customary Philippine image of sun-drenched beaches and glorious coral reefs. There are beaches to visit in and around **Subic Bay** and **San Fernando**, but the region's main interest lies inland. Home to tribal minorities, the area's high, rugged mountains and pine forests offer a rare opportunity to escape the tropical heat. The city of **Baguio** is the capital of this region, beyond which the rough **Halsema Road** links up many of the mountain areas, including the beautiful village of **Sagada** and the mighty rice terraces of **Banaue**. At the southern edge of the mountains stands **Mt Pinatubo**, one of the world's most famous volcanoes, following its spectacular 1991 eruption. Nearby, the healthy **rain forests** and relatively tame wildlife of Subic Bay offer a rare opportunity for visitors to experience this type of environment.

On the northwest coast of Luzon is the town of **Vigan**, one of the oldest Spanish settlements in the country and the best preserved of all. Here, an entire section of the town consists of streets lined with Castilian houses, and it is possible to stay in several old Spanish villas.

The most northerly point of the Philippines lies in the **Batanes Islands**, closer to Taiwan than to mainland Luzon. Wild, remote and storm-battered, the landscape and high cliffs of these islands have been compared with those of Ireland.

Don't Miss

*** Subic Forest: accessible tropical lowland rain forest, with reasonably tame wildlife.
*** Sagada: a village high in the mountains, with walking trails and caves to explore.
** Rice terraces of Banaue: 2000-year-old rice terraces high on the mountain slopes.
** Hundred Islands: a group of small islands surrounded by clear, shallow sea.
** Batanes Islands: wild, remote islands lined with dramatic scenery.
* Vigan: the best preserved of all the old Spanish towns in the Philippines.

Opposite: *Rice terraces carved into the Cordillera Central mountains.*

Above: The new Subic Yacht Club is a powerful symbol of the Subic Bay Freeport's new importance in the leisure and tourism business.

BATAAN AND ZAMBALES

The Bataan Peninsula forms the western wall of Manila Bay, protecting the capital from the westerly winds of the South China Sea. To the north lies Zambales province, composed mostly of the Zambales Mountains and a narrow coastal plain. The most important development in the area is **Subic Bay**, along with the adjacent town of **Olongapo**.

Subic Bay **

About 130km (80 miles) from Manila, the southeastern chunk of this large enclosed bay was an American naval base until the US military pulled out of the Philippines in 1992. It was originally developed as a naval port by the Spanish, but was taken over by the Americans in 1899 during the Spanish–American War. It was occupied by the Japanese during World War II, but returned to American control in 1945. During the Vietnam War it became the USA's largest overseas military base.

When the Americans pulled out, economic disaster loomed for the local people, but instead the site was turned into a freeport and economic zone, a move which has been remarkably successful. Today, the urban part of **Subic Bay Freeport** (SBF) is a modern town, still with many American trappings. Because of the port's duty-free status, entry and exit are controlled: upon arrival you will need to do some form filling, and when you leave you may be searched.

For the general visitor, the main attractions include an 18-hole **golf course**, three **beaches** and the **forest**. For watersports enthusiasts, this is a great place for **windsurfing**, especially during the southwest monsoon (June–October), and is one of the Philippines' two major **wreck diving** locations. The bay is strewn with wrecks and it is possible to dive onto several old warships.

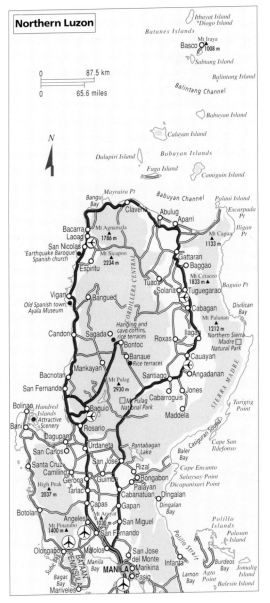

Northern Luzon

0   87.5 km

0   65.6 miles

N

Itbayat Island
Diogo Island
Batanes Islands
Basco   Mt Iraya   1008 m
Sabtang Island
Balintang Island
Balintang Channel

Babuyan Island

Calayan Island

Dalupiri Island   *Babuyan Islands*
Fuga Island
Camiguin Island

Mayraira Pt   *Babuyan Channel*   *Palaui Island*
Bangui
Bay   Claveria   Abulug   *Escarpada Pt*
Aparri
Bacarra   Mt Agnamala   *Iligan Pt*
Laoag   1786 m   Mt Cagua
San Nicolas   1133 m
'Earthquake Baroque'   Mt Sicapoo
Spanish church   2234 m
Espiritu   Gattaran
Baggao
Mt Cetaceo
1833 m ▲   *Baguio Pt*
Vigan   Tuao   Solana   Tuguegarao
Old Spanish town/   Bangued
Ayala Museum   Cabagan   *Divilican Bay*
Mt Palanan
Candon   Sagada   Hanging and   Ilagan   1212 m
cave coffins,   Roxas   Northern Sierra
rice terraces   Madre □
Bontoc   Natural Park
Banaue   Cauayan
Bacnotan   Mankayan   Rice terraces
Santiago   Angadanan
San Fernando   Mt Pulag
2930 m   Jones
Bolinao   *Hundred*   □Mt Pulag   Cabarroguis   *Tarigtig Point*
Islands   Baguio   *National Park*
• *Attractive*   Maddela
Bani   *Scenery*
Dagupan   Rosario
San Carlos   Urdaneta   *Pantabagan Lake*   *Cape San Ildefonso*
Santa Cruz   San Jose   Baler
Camiling   Rizal   *Bay*
High Peak   Gerona   Guimba   Bongabon   *Cape Encanto*
2037 m   Palayan   *Salaysay Point*
Tarlac   *Dicapanisari Point*
Capas   Cabanatuan   Dingalan
Botolan   Gapan
Angeles   Mt Arayat   San Miguel   *Dingalan Bay*
Mt Pinatubo   1030 m ▲
1400 m ▲   San Fernando
Olongapo   Malolos   *Polillo Islands*
Subic Bay   San Jose   *Palasan Island*
Manila   del Monte
BATAAN   *Bay*   Marikina   Infanta   *Burdeos*   *Jomalig Island*
Bagac   MANILA   Pasig   *Lamon*   *Agta*   *Bay*   *Point*
Bay   Mariveles   *Balesin Island*

CORDILLERA CENTRAL

SIERRA MADRE

PENINSULA

Polillo Strait

Casiguran Sound

SUNKEN WRECKS

As a naval base set up at the end of the 19th century, Subic Bay has seen plenty of action. Numerous wrecks litter the floor of the bay, and several are now used for wreck diving. The oldest of these is the *San Quintin*, sunk by the Spanish in 1898 in an attempt to block part of the bay's entrance and prevent an American attack. All the other wrecks date from World War II, the biggest being the ex-*USS New York*, a large battleship that was scuppered by the Americans in 1941. Other wrecks include the *Oryoku Maru*, a Japanese cruise liner sunk by US aircraft in 1944, and the *Seian Maru*, a Japanese freighter sunk in 1945.

Below: *A member of Subic's Jungle Environmental Survival Training Center shows how to make fire without matches.*

Opposite: *A resort and beach near Barrio Barretto in Subic Bay.*
Below: *Light aircraft for hire at Clark Field, with Mt Pinatubo in the distance.*

Subic Watershed Forest ★★★

The 10,000ha (25,000-acre) forest surrounding Subic Bay is one of the last remaining areas of tropical lowland rain forest in Luzon and, together with forest outside the SBF, makes up Subic–Bataan Natural Park, one of the country's highest priority protected areas. Roads crisscross the forest, making access easy, and with almost no hunting for the past 100 years the wildlife has become quite tame. Macaques are a common sight, and there are also forest birds, many of them unique to the Philippines. One of the major attractions is a huge colony of **fruit bats** that roost during the daytime in tall trees next to the residential area of Cubi. A viewpoint on a steep hillside allows visitors a close view of the bats at tree-top height.

Above Cubi is **JEST**, the Jungle Environment Survival Training camp. Originally set up to train soldiers in jungle survival techniques, its members, mostly from the **Aeta** tribe that live in the forest, now offer the same services to visitors. Most settle for a two-hour tour that takes in such skills as making a dinner set from bamboo, identifying edible and medicinal plants, navigating, and starting a fire without matches.

In another part of the forest is **Pamulaklakin**, a model Aeta village, where the locals put on cultural shows, and from where guided hikes through the forest begin.

The wildest parts of the forest lie within the **Naval Magazine** area (Navmag for short). Roads penetrate this area too, reaching out to its many disused ammunition bunkers, but access is restricted. Anyone wishing to enter the Navmag needs a permit, obtainable from the SBF's Ecology Centre, and to go hiking you must be accompanied by a ranger. Furthermore, there is no public transport in the Navmag; you need your own vehicle.

Olongapo *

Situated immediately outside the main gates to Subic Bay, the town of Olongapo has always provided labour for the base and, in turn, the SBF. Apart from a number of restaurants and bars, the town itself has very little of interest, although it does make rather a good base from which to explore the rest of the Subic Bay area as its hotels are considerably cheaper than those inside the SBF. North of Olongapo, further into the bay but outside the SBF, are a number of very attractive sandy beaches, particularly those at the village of **Barrio Barretto**.

Angeles and Mt Pinatubo *

Approximately 80km (50 miles) to the northeast of Olongapo is Angeles, which until 1992 was the site of **Clark Airforce Base**, another major centre for the US military. Situated right at the foot of Mt Pinatubo, both the military base and the town were devastated by the volcano's 1991 eruption. Since the American withdrawal **Clark Field** (as it is nowadays called), following Subic's example, has become a duty-free economic zone, encouraging industries to move in and touting its potential as a major new international airport. In the town outside Clark Field, business is booming as before, and the bars and brothels that once catered to the American GIs are now attracting those tourists who travel up here from Manila specifically for the nightlife.

Thankfully, Angeles does have another role. It is the starting point for treks into Pinatubo's lahar fields, sometimes going as far as the crater rim. In Clark Field you can also hire an airplane for sightseeing tours around Pinatubo. Such flights must be undertaken early in the morning before thermal currents build up.

SUBIC WATERSHED FOREST

This tropical lowland rain forest is one of the few remaining areas of its type in Luzon. Protected by the American military when this was a naval base, it is now a vitally important nature reserve. The forest was partly damaged by Mt Pinatubo's eruption, but already the only reminders of that are the unusually large numbers of dead trees and the open canopy. Some of the best forest is in the Naval Magazine area (where old ammunition bunkers can still be seen), and here the forest comes right down to the shoreline, to include some rare beach forest which merges with mangroves.

CENTRAL WEST COAST

About 90km (55 miles) north of Angeles you come to the coast of the **Lingayen Gulf**. Around here are a number of locations worth visiting. To the west are the **Hundred Islands**, while to the east lie the beautiful beaches of the **San Fernando** area.

Hundred Islands **

A scattering of limestone islands in a shallow azure sea, this area has been designated a National Recreation Area. The nearest large town is **Alaminos**, reachable from Olongapo/Subic via the picturesque Zambales coast road. From Angeles or Manila you would follow the congested main highway. Alaminos is a chaotic town, but fortunately there is no need to stay there. Instead, continue on another 5km (3 miles) to the coastal village of **Lucap**, where boats can be hired for a tour of the islands. The shoreline at Lucap is not pretty either, with its scrappy hotel development and half filled-in fish ponds. Boats to tour the Hundred Islands can be hired either from the jetty or one of the waterside hotels.

Most of the islands are tiny and impossible to land on, but a few have beaches where boats can come ashore. **Governor's Island** is the first of these. Here a footpath climbs to the summit of a hill, from which there is a good view of the little archipelago. Further out is **Children's Island**, quite a large place with more footpaths and views. There are cottages to let here; there is no electricity and you have to bring all your own food and water, but a kerosene lamp is provided. One of the outermost islands is **Quezon Island**, which because of its beautiful sandy beach attracts the most visitors.

San Fernando (La Union) *

Not to be confused with the inland town of San Fernando just north of Manila and in Pampanga province, this coastal town is known for its beaches that stretch along the coast north and south. Most beach life is concentrated around the village of **Bauang**, approximately 10km (6 miles) south. Here a string of well-developed beach resorts cater to people coming up from Manila at the weekends. Though it is a pleasant spot, the sand is rather grey and the beach is so crowded with boats (mostly there for tourism, not fishing) that at high tide it is often necessary to walk in the water!

Just a few kilometres north of San Fernando, at the village of **San Juan**, things are completely different. The sand is still rather grey here, but the beach is huge, both wide and several kilometres long, and pounded by surf. At the southern end, where the surf is at its best, are several surf camps. Along the entire beach there has so far been very little development, and the tiny handful of resorts are separated by huge distances.

Opposite: *A rocky islet, one of the many that make up Hundred Islands.*
Below: *Boats fill the beach at Bauang, the main beach resort in northern Luzon.*

Babuyan Islands

Abulug
San Nicolas
Baggao
Vigan
Roxas
San Fernando   Angadanan
Baguio

Below: *Crisologo St is lined with Spanish houses that recall the colonial past.*

THE NORTHWEST

The northwest is a very pleasant rural area, the journey northwards from San Fernando passing through an agricultural landscape rich in rice, maize and tobacco. This was the homeland of the dictator **Ferdinand Marcos**, and he is still something of a hero in these parts. The first, and most interesting, town in the area is **Vigan**, an old Spanish town.

Vigan **

Situated 139km (90 miles) north of San Fernando and 400km (250 miles) from Manila, Vigan was an important port long before the Spanish arrived in 1572. Today it is known as the fourth-oldest Spanish settlement in the country and without doubt the best preserved. One entire section of the city consists of nothing but cobbled streets lined with ancient Spanish houses. One street in particular, **Crisologo Street**, is of importance as it is lined with furniture workshops – as well as one place that still weaves with a traditional hand-loom. Motorized vehicles are not allowed in this area, the only transport being horse-drawn carriages, or *calesa*.

At the northern end of the old town is the beautiful **St Paul's Cathedral**, with next door the **Archbishop's Palace**. Nearby is the **Ayala Museum** which traces much of Vigan's history (open Mon–Fri 08:30–11:30 and 13:30–16:30). The museum is housed in the birthplace of José Burgos, an early Filipino patriot executed in 1872 by the Spanish. At the southwestern end of town are several **pottery workshops**, where it is possible to watch large *burnay* pots being made, traditionally used for the storage of foodstuffs. In the centre of the old town there are a number of old villas that can be visited,

of which the most beautiful is **Villa Angela**. Here, the elegant furnishings are a pleasing blend of Spanish, Chinese and Malay. Villa Angela also doubles up as a hotel; one of the management's proud boasts is that Tom Cruise once stayed here!

Beyond Vigan the coast road continues through the city of **Laoag**, passing along the way the **Paoay**

Above: *A view of the Cordillera Central mountains seen near Baguio, with Mt Pulag (2930m), highest mountain on Luzon, in the distance.*

Church and also Marcos' birthplace at **Batac**. Further north, there are some remote beaches at **Pagudpud**, shortly before **Mayraira Point**, the most northerly point of mainland Luzon.

CORDILLERA CENTRAL

This mountainous region is the very heart of northern Luzon, to which many visitors flock, if only to get away from the lowland heat! The people here, many of them from tribal minorities, are proud and independent, having for many years successfully resisted control by the Spanish and Americans. Today, with their stupendous scenery and unique culture, the mountains offer a view of the Philippines that is radically diferent from the usual one of sand and surf.

Baguio **

Most visitors to the Philippines begin their tour of the mountains in Baguio, the capital of Benguet province and by far the largest settlement in the Cordillera. At an altitude of some 1500m (4900ft) the air is pleasantly cool, though in the downtown area it is hard to find much truth in the tourist literature's claims for Baguio's relaxing atmosphere, views and scented pine trees. Actually, the city centre is just as congested and polluted as any other city in the Philippines.

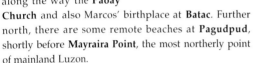

> **DIEGO AND GABRIELA SILANG**
>
> Diego Silang led a rebellion in the Vigan area in December 1762, inspired by an announcement by the British (who had just taken over Manila) that the natives should be left to run their own lives. However, the Spanish bishop of Vigan, Bernardo Ustariz, hired an assassin, Miguel Vicos, who killed Silang in May 1763. The remaining rebels, led by Diego's wife Gabriela Silang, continued the rebellion but were eventually caught and executed. Gabriela Silang was the last to die – she was hanged in Vigan on 20 September 1763.

Above: *The Cordillera's vegetable farms, such as this one on the slopes of Mt Pulag, supply most of the Philippines' temperate fruit and vegetables, from strawberries to cabbages, carrots and potatoes.*

MT PULAG

Northeast of Baguio stands Mt Pulag, at 2930m (9610ft) the highest mountain in Luzon, and often wrongly claimed to be the second-highest in the Philippines. A national park, the mountain's highest areas are covered with grass and dwarf bamboo less than a metre (3ft) high, while a little lower is a large area of dense mossy forest, characterized by short, gnarled trees draped in moss and lichen. Below the mossy forest is a forest of Benguet pines, though this has been badly damaged by encroaching vegetable farms.

That does not mean that the downtown area is not enjoyable. **Session Road**, the main street, is a colourful and lively place with a range of shops and restaurants, while at the bottom of the hill the **city market** is one of the most interesting in the country. Nearby, **Burnham Park** with its boating lake is a welcome city centre oasis.

To enjoy the feeling of being in a mountain resort it is important to stay in one of the hotels on the eastern side of the city, where parks and pine forests merge with the housing. Here, the **Botanical Garden** and **Wright Park** are pleasant forested places, while further out is **Mines View Park**, a lookout point with a spectacular view across the mountains. This is also a good place to pick up some **mountain handicrafts**, as there are many stalls selling an array of weaving and woodcarving products.

Most impressive is **Club John Hay**, a huge rambling park containing a golf course and country club, tennis courts, restaurants, a hotel and attractive woodlands. Originally called Camp John Hay, this was another centre for the US military, this time a recreation facility.

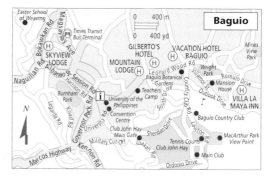

Places of interest to the north and northwest of the city include the **St Louis University Silver Shop**, where visitors can watch silversmiths at work, and the **Easter School of Weaving**, where the same applies for people working on traditional hand-looms. The end products can be bought at both these places.

The Halsema Road **

Linking Baguio with the town of **Bontoc**, the capital of Mountain province and about 130km (95 miles) to the north, this is the most spectacular road in the Philippines, offering superb views of the Cordillera mountains, including Mt Pulag (2930m; 9610ft), the tallest mountain on Luzon. The highest point reached by the road itself is on a pass at 2255m (7396ft) – the highest point on any road in the country – which is about a third of the way towards Bontoc. Unfortunately, the Halsema does not offer a gentle ride, since most of it is unpaved and in very bad condition. Even in the dry season the journey takes seven hours, and in the rains it may be completely impassable.

Sagada ***

A left turn off the Halsema Road just a few kilometres before Bontoc leads high up into the mountains to one of the Cordillera's gems: the village of Sagada, nestling in forest at an altitude of 1400m (4600ft). With its cool air and relaxed atmosphere, this is a genuine mountain retreat. Hiking trails head off to a number of mountain peaks, waterfalls and caves. The last of these are especially interesting since the people here have traditionally buried their dead in caves or in hanging coffins attached to the sides of cliffs. It is still quite a common practice today.

Below: *Hanging coffins attached to a cliff in Echo Valley, Sagada.*

A LIFE APART

The people of the Batanes Islands have long lived an isolated life. About 230km (143 miles) from the Luzon mainland, 650km (406 miles) from Manila and 250km (160 miles) from Taiwan, the people here live completely surrounded by deep oceans. Until regular flights started just a couple of years ago, the islanders were reliant on an infrequent freighter for essential supplies and the export of their main products – beef and goat's meat. Life continues to be simple, but was greatly modernized with the arrival in the 1990s of electricity, motor transport and television.

Opposite: *A view along the coast of Batan Island towards Mt Iraya (1008m).*
Below: *A tiny farming village forms a tight cluster of houses in the Cordillera mountains near Banaue.*

Unfortunately, vandalism has forced the locals to close some of the caves, but one of the most interesting areas to explore, quite close to the village, is **Echo Valley**. This narrow gorge contains a number of caves as well as a cliff to which are attached several coffins. Although only one of the caves contains coffins, another is unusual for having an **underground river** flowing out of its mouth.

There are many caves more remote than these, but to explore them you need to hire a guide. This can be arranged at the tourist desk in Sagada's municipal office.

Banaue and the Rice Terraces**

About 340km (200 miles) north of Manila and 150km (95 miles) from Baguio, the 2000-year-old rice terraces that cover the mountainsides around Banaue are touted as one of the must-see places of northern Luzon. With more than a little hyperbole they have been called the Eighth Wonder of the World, but, even if they are not as spectacular as the tourist brochures would have the world believe, they are nevertheless beautiful and quite remarkable. The terraces immediately above the town of Banaue and visible from the **Banaue View Point** are the most accessible, but are less stunning than those around **Batad**, a village about 15km (10 miles) to the east by road and then needing a two-hour hike to reach.

BATANES ISLANDS

This remote cluster of 10 islands represents the most northerly point of the Philippines, lying between the Luzon mainland and Taiwan, 650km (390 miles) north of Manila. Right in the path of virtually every typhoon that comes along, the islands are storm-battered and for much of the year barely accessible.

Three of the islands, **Batan**, **Itbayat** and **Sabtang**, are inhabited, the total population being about 14,000. Most of the people belong to the **Ivatan** ethnic group, with their own language and customs quite distinct from the mainland. Architecture is unique too, with thick stone walls and heavy thatching adapted to the harsh climate. The main town is **Basco**, on Batan, lying at the foot of 1008m (3306ft) Mt Iraya, an inactive volcano. Basco is a lovely little town with almost no traffic and very friendly people. Apart from Mt Iraya, much of the landscape consists of rolling hills on which cattle and goats graze, while the coast is a mixture of sheer cliffs and gentle bays with rocky islets offshore. Sabtang is similar, though the lifestyle here is more traditional than on Batan. Itbayat, though the largest island, is thinly populated and very difficult to reach.

These islands are for lovers of the remote and the outdoors. A number of hiking trails crisscross Batan, including one up Mt Iraya. You will need a guide on some of the more remote trails.

Northern Luzon and Batanes Islands at a Glance

BEST TIMES TO VISIT

For lowland areas in northern Luzon, weather patterns are the same as for Manila: rain June–October, dry December–May. April and May are the hottest months. In the mountains the rains last from April or May to November.

GETTING THERE

There are daily **flights** from Manila to Baguio and Subic Bay, and five times a week to Laoag. Buses run from Manila to Angeles, San Fernando, Olongapo, Alaminos, Vigan, Laoag, Baguio and Banaue.

GETTING AROUND

Frequent **bus** services go from Olongapo up the Zambales coast to Alaminos, and from Angeles to Alaminos. Take a **jeepney** or **tricycle** to Lucap. Buses run along the coast from Alaminos to San Fernando, though you may have to change in Dagupan en route. From San Fernando, there are buses to Vigan, Laoag and Baguio. To go from Baguio to Sagada, take a bus to Bontoc and then backtrack by jeepney to Sagada. To continue to Banaue, travel to Bontoc, and then take a bus to Banaue. Self-drive **cars** hired in Manila can be driven over this entire route, though be aware that the Halsema Road may exact a heavy toll – at least be prepared for punctures. Set off with a full tank; filling stations are few and far between.

WHERE TO STAY

Subic Bay
LUXURY
Subic Legenda Hotel and Casino, Waterfront Rd, Subic Bay Freeport, tel: (047) 252-1888. A modern hotel in SBF's commercial district.
Crown Peak Gardens Leisure Hotels and Convention Center, Cubi, Subic Bay Freeport, tel: (047) 252-3144, fax: (047) 252-6658. A large complex set in the residential area, surrounded by forest.

Olongapo
MID-RANGE
By the Sea Hotel and Resort, 99 National Highway, Barrio Baretto, Olongapo City, tel: (047) 222-4560. A beachside resort north of the city.

Angeles
MID-RANGE
Swagman Narra Hotel, SL Orosa St, Diamond Subdivision, Angeles City, Pampanga, tel: (0455) 602-5133, fax: (0455) 602-9467.

Hundred Islands
MID-RANGE
Maxine by the Sea Lodge and Restaurant, Lucap, Alaminos, Pangasinan. Simple rooms and a good restaurant; views of Hundred Islands.

San Fernando (La Union)
LUXURY
Cabana Beach Resort, Bauang, La Union, tel: (072) 412824, fax: (072) 414496.

Puerto de San Juan, Ili Sur, San Juan, La Union, tel/fax: (072) 242-3330. A new resort, right on the beach.

MID-RANGE
China Sea Beach Resort, Paringao, Bauang, La Union, tel: (072) 414821, fax: (072) 242-0822, e-mail: chinasea@net.com.ph. Beachside development of cottages with a pool and restaurant.

Vigan
MID-RANGE
El Juliana Hotel, 5 Liberation corner Quirino Blvd, Vigan, Ilocos Sur, tel: (077) 722-2994. Attractive hotel in the old town, with a pool and restaurant.

BUDGET
Villa Angela, 25 Quirino Blvd, Vigan, Ilocos Sur. Beautiful old Spanish villa with antique furnishings; no restaurant.

Baguio
MID-RANGE
Mount Crest Hotel, Legarda Road, Baguio City, Benguet, tel: (074) 442-3324, fax: (074) 443-9273, e-mail: mch@bgo.cyberspace.com.ph. A hotel just outside the city centre, close to Burnham Park. Has its own cyber café.
Vacation Hotel Baguio, 45 Leonard Wood Rd, Baguio City, Benguet, tel: (074) 442-4545, fax: (074) 442-3144. A hillside hotel surrounded by pine forest, close to the Botanical Garden and Wright Park.

Northern Luzon and Batanes Islands at a Glance

BUDGET
Gilberto's Hotel, 43 CM Recto St, Navy Rd, Baguio City, Benguet, tel: (074) 442-4357, fax: (074) 442-8036. An old-fashioned hotel, huge rooms.
Mountain Lodge, 27 Leonard Wood Rd, Baguio City, Benguet, tel: (074) 442-4544. Old hotel, near Botanical Garden.

Sagada
MID-RANGE
Sagada Prime Hotel, Sagada, Mountain Province. Booking office, tel: (074) 442-2622.

BUDGET
Olahbinan Café and Resthouse, Poblacion, Sagada, Mountain Province.
Rocky Valley Inn, Sagada, Mountain Province.

Banaue
MID-RANGE
Banaue Hotel and Youth Hostel, Banaue, Ifugao, tel: (073) 386-4087, fax: (073) 386-4048. Banaue's largest hotel.

BUDGET
Fairview Inn, Banaue, Ifugao. A pleasant and large house.
People's Bakery Lodge and Restaurant, Banaue, Ifugao. Guesthouse with restaurant.

Basco
BUDGET
Mama Lilys, Basco, Batanes.
Ivatan Lodge, Basco, Batanes. Accommodation is limited in the Batanes Islands, and there are few telephones to aid

advance booking. Meals are usually eaten at the lodge.

WHERE TO EAT

Subic Bay
Feng Huang, Dewey Avenue, Subic Bay Freeport, tel: (047) 252-1888. Chinese food.
Casa Ilongga, Royal Subic Mall, Subic Bay Freeport, tel: (047) 252-3864. Filipino food.

Olongapo
Rama Mahal Bar and Restaurant, 41 Fendler St, corner Magsaysay Drive, Olongapo City, Bataan, tel: (047) 223-9960. Indian restaurant.

Baguio
Café by the Ruins, 23 Chuntog St, Baguio City, Benguet, tel: (074) 442-4010. A wonderful vegetarian restaurant.
Sizzling Plate, 116 Session Rd, Baguio City, Benguet, tel: (074) 442-4219. Steak house.

SHOPPING

Duty-free shopping is available to foreign visitors in Subic Bay Freeport, but only within 48 hours of their arrival in the Philippines. Your passport will be checked before purchases can be made.

For **handicrafts**, Baguio offers the best choice, especially of **woodcarvings** and **weaving**. The best of the latter is available at the Easter School of Weaving.

TOURS AND EXCURSIONS

Tours of many parts of northern Luzon, including hiking in the Mt Pinatubo area, can be arranged through Swagman Travel (offices in Manila, Olangapo, Angeles, Bauang and Baguio). Arrange with your hotel for tours around the SBF.

USEFUL CONTACTS

Department of Tourism, Cordillera Administrative Region, DOT-Complex, Gov. Pack Rd, Baguio City, tel: (074) 442-6708, fax: (074) 442-8848.
Department of Tourism Regional Office I, Mabanag Justice Hall, San Fernando, La Union, tel: (072) 412411, fax: (072) 412098.
Swagman Travel, 411 A. Flores St, Ermita, Manila, tel: (02) 523-8541, fax: (02) 522-3663, e-mail: bookings@swaggy.com.
Laoag Int. Airlines, Andy's Bldg, Ruzal St, Laoag City, 2090, Tel: (077) 772-1793.

BAGUIO	J	F	M	A	M	J	J	A	S	O	N	D
AVERAGE TEMP. °F	64	64	66	68	68	68	66	66	68	68	66	64
AVERAGE TEMP. °C	18	18	19	20	20	20	20	19	19	20	19	18
RAINFALL ins.	0.5	0.3	1	3.5	13.6	19	31.8	36	24.8	14.6	4.6	0.9
RAINFALL mm	12	8	26	89	346	484	808	912	628	371	116	23
DAYS OF RAINFALL	3	2	4	9	19	22	26	28	24	16	8	4

4
Southern Luzon and Mindoro

Southern Luzon consists of a narrow peninsula stretching for over 600km (375 miles) southeastwards from Manila. It is a highly volcanic land, with several active volcanoes – including both **Taal** and **Mayon**, the country's most active and dangerous volcanoes – and innumerable others that are dormant. Taal stands at the centre of **Calabarzon**, an area just south of Manila that is a weekend playground for Manila residents. Here can be found hiking trails, hot springs, waterfalls and beaches, all within easy reach of the capital.

Mt Mayon is the dominant feature of the **Bicol** region, close to the southeastern tip of Luzon, and it looms ominously over the city of **Legaspi**. Its near-perfect cone, which sweeps upwards from the sea to a pointed smouldering peak, is one of the most recognizable images of the Philippines, and for hikers a climb to its summit is one of the country's greatest challenges. There are a number of other climbable volcanoes in the area, including **Mt Bulusan**. Off the coast, near the town of **Donsol**, it has recently become possible to swim with whale sharks.

Mindoro is a wild and mountainous island to the south of Luzon, easily accessible from Calabarzon. Much of the island is still poorly developed, and tourism concentrates around the resort of **Puerto Galera**, a beautiful peninsula at the northern tip. Off Mindoro's west coast lies **Apo Reef**, an important site for turtles and other marine life, which in recent years has become a popular site for divers.

DON'T MISS

*** Puerto Galera: coves and beaches, superb diving.
** Mt Mayon: the most active volcano in the Philippines, famous for its almost perfect cone.
** Mt Bulusan: an active volcano, with a pleasant lake and rain forest at its feet.
** Los Banos and Mt Makiling: views of Laguna de Bay, walks in Makiling's forest, and the Philippine Raptor Center.
* Lake Taal and Taal Volcano: views of the caldera lake and the island on which the Taal volcano sits.

Opposite: *Even in downtown Legaspi you can see the summit of Mt Mayon.*

Right: *Lake Taal, a huge flooded volcanic caldera, presents an idyllic view from Tagaytay high up on the caldera's rim. Taal Island, however, in the centre of the view, is the site of one of the Philippines' most deadly and most active volcanoes.*

CALABARZON

Calabarzon – an acronym for the provinces of Cavite, Laguna, Batangas, Rizal and Quezon – is a densely populated region immediately to the south of Manila. A large proportion of it is covered by **Laguna de Bay**, the country's largest lake. Waterfalls and hot springs are dotted around these mountains, while along the coasts are numerous beaches and dive sites.

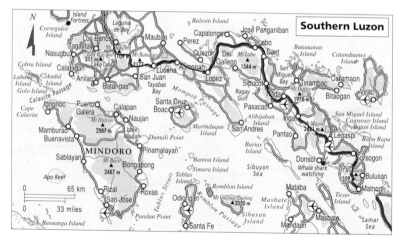

Tagaytay and Taal Volcano **

Some 70km (45 miles) south of central Manila lies Taal Lake, a flooded caldera that forms the remains of an ancient massive volcano. In the centre of the lake is an island on which stands Taal volcano, said to be one of the world's smallest but deadliest volcanoes. The lake was once an enclosed bay on the coast, but a series of eruptions in the 18th century sealed the entrance and turned it into a lake. The last big eruption took place in 1911.

For a spectacular view of the lake and volcano island, head for **Tagaytay**, a town on the northwestern rim of the caldera. At an altitude of 760m (2500ft), night time can be especially cool. The town is spread out, and in itself not very interesting. Apart from the view, there is horse riding and also a golf course, while the local volcanology unit has an interesting exhibition.

Boat trips across the lake and hiking on the the volcano island, right down into the active crater (where there is another small lake) can be organized at the little towns of Talisay, Leynes or Laurel on the lake's northern shore, or San Nicolas on the south side.

THE TAAL ERUPTION OF 1911

One of Taal's worst eruptions in recent history began on 29 January 1911, sending a column of smoke and ash high into the sky, and avalanches of volcanic rock and debris across Taal Island. Many of the farmers tilling the island's rich volcanic soils were killed by the blast, while those that escaped on their boats were drowned by tidal waves that swept the lake. Over 1300 people died on that one day.

Below: *The crested serpent eagle is spread across much of south and southeast Asia. In the Philippines it is quite a common sight.*

Los Banos and Mt Makiling **

The hot spring resort of Los Banos lies approximately 65km (40 miles) south of Manila, on the southern shore of Laguna de Bay and at the northern foot of Mt Makiling. Hot springs bubbling out from the base of this dormant volcano are the attraction for many Filipinos, and there are a number of resorts scattered along the main road towards Manila. The old part of the town is a quiet, pleasant collection of old houses, with lovely views of the lake and the thousands of fish farms that reach out over the shallow waters.

Above the town, on the lower slopes of Makiling, stands a campus of the **University of the Philippines**, housing mostly forestry, agricultural and biology departments. The surroundings are beautiful, with parklands covered with rain forest trees. On the campus is the **Makiling Botanical Garden**, which consists mostly of dense rain forest through which a few roads and many footpaths have been cut. Among the trees is the **Philippine Raptor Center**, a home for injured or confiscated Philippine birds of prey. Besides an extremely tame crested serpent eagle, this place provides a very rare opportunity to see the world's second-largest raptor, the **Philippine eagle**, of which two live here.

Above the Botanical Garden the campus road becomes a track that climbs the mountain to its summit at 1144m (3752ft). If taking this route, be sure to take plenty of water with you and also to register with the guard at the start of the track. The hike up and down takes all day and is through dense rain forest. Though now classed as a forest reserve, Mt Makiling was one of the country's first national parks, declared in 1933 and protected by the university ever since.

Mt Banahaw **

Southeast of Laguna de Bay stands Mt Banahaw, an active volcano that, with its three peaks and impressive height of 2177m (7141ft), easily dominates the landscape. Partially forested, the mountain has a number of hot

Right: *Fish farms and traps spread across the shallow waters of Laguna de Bay, lit by the light of sunrise and seen from Los Banos on the southern shore. The country's largest lake, it is intensively used by the huge local population (which includes parts of Manila), with both pollution and fishing threatening the lake's survival.*

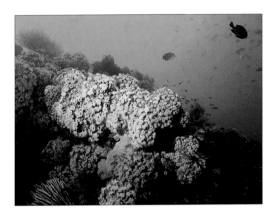

Left: Tubastraea *cup corals put on a golden show on a reef near Maricaban Island off the Calumpan Peninsula, Batangas. This area, reached via dive centres in the village of Anilao, offers Manila's nearest good quality diving.*

springs, waterfalls and caves, and has become known as a sacred mountain. During Holy Week, just before Easter, thousands of people make a pilgrimage to the summit.

There are several trails up the mountain, each making for one of the three peaks, though the most used route starts from the town of San Pablo, on the mountain's northwestern flank. You will need to take all your own equipment and food, and hire a guide at the national park office in the village of Santa Lucia at the trailhead. To the summit and back is an arduous three-day trek.

Beaches and Dive Resorts *

About 40km (25 miles) west of Tagaytay, some 110km (70 miles) from Manila, are the towns of **Nasugbu** and **Matabungkay**, the nearest beaches to the capital. Although not the country's most beautiful beaches, they are perfectly enjoyable, with several kilometres of sand, and are easily reached by road.

For diving it is better to head further south, especially to the **Calumpan Peninsula** near Batangas, where most dive resorts are centred around the village of **Anilao**. Here, and most especially around the nearby island of Maricaban, is some excellent diving, with a wealth of coral and fish species to be seen. Note that Anilao has no beach and there is very little for non-divers to do.

VOLCANOLOGY

The Philippines' volcanoes are studied and monitored by the Philippine Institute of Volcanology and Seismology (PHIVOLCS), based in Manila. Monitoring stations set up close to several of the country's 22 active volcanoes watch for possible eruptions through measurements of localized earthquake activity and gas emissions. Increasing numbers of earthquakes, which come progressively closer to the earth's surface and more closely aligned with the volcano's base, are a clear indication of an approaching eruption. Knowing exactly when the eruption will take place, however, is still extremely difficult to predict.

Right: *Teeing-off across a ravine at the Ponderosa Golf Club, in the hills high above Puerto Galera.*
Opposite: *Boats drawn up on the sand at Big La Laguna Beach, Puerto Galera, Mindoro.*

KING COCONUT

It is hard to find a crop more versatile than the coconut palm. Drinking its milk and eating its flesh are just the tip of the iceberg. Not only is the tree itself valuable for construction materials, but the nuts have a huge range of uses. These include the production of coconut oils, copra, charcoal, activated carbon, vinegar, plant culture media, growth hormones, laundry soap and detergent. Coconut is a major crop in the Philippines, an estimated 285 million palms occupying 3.2 million ha (8 million acres) and earning US$700 million annually. The country's palms account for two-thirds of the world's coconut oil, over 80 per cent of which is exported to Europe and North America.

MINDORO

This wild and mountainous island has been little explored by visitors, and although a trickle of divers head for the west coast town of **Sablayan** in order to reach the dive sites of **Apo Reef**, the great majority of visitors head for just one place – **Puerto Galera** – situated at the northernmost tip of Mindoro.

Puerto Galera ★★★

A two-hour ferry journey from the port of Batangas on the southern tip of Calabarzon, Puerto Galera is one of the Philippines' most popular and most beautiful resort areas. Upon arrival from Batangas, the ferry enters **Muelle Bay**, a landlocked stretch of water enclosed by a peninsula and a cluster of islands, all vivid green in their covering of coconut palms. Sandy beaches line the shore and yachts lie at anchor close to the wharf that marks arrival at Puerto Galera town. From here, new arrivals are taken by *banca* or jeepney out to any one of numerous beaches lying east and west of the town.

The most popular destinations in the area are the beaches at **Big** and **Small La Laguna** and **Sabang**, which line the outermost point of the Puerto Galera Peninsula to the east of town. To the west lie several more beaches, including **White Beach**, **Aninuan** and **Talipanan**, which are generally less developed than the first three. Puerto Galera is one of the country's prime dive sites, a large area of coral reefs having been protected in a **marine sanctuary** for many years. There is a great array of hard and soft corals, basket sponges, sea fans and fish life, and the many dive operators all offer training courses.

Inland, there is a **golf course**, a remarkable place hacked out of the steep terrain and dense forests, which at one point involves teeing off across a ravine. There are also a couple of waterfalls, both within walking distance of Talipanan and Aninuan beaches, while longer hikes lead to villages inhabited by the **Mangyan** people, Mindoro's aboriginals.

> ### PUERTO GALERA
> ### DIVE SITES
>
> Most of the best dive sites are within or close to the marine reserve, which stretches along the northern coastline of the peninsula. Some of the dives are over shallow coral gardens that snorkellers can enjoy too, but others are deep and in some places involve strong currents. On the shallower dives a wide range of corals, basket sponges and reef fish can be seen. In the deepest waters, at around 40m (130ft), sharks may be encountered. There are at least 24 dive sites, with names as varied as Manila Channel, Monkey Wreck, Sabang Point, Ernie's Cave, Hole in the Wall and The Fish Bowl.

Apo Reef **

Lying about 35km (20 miles) off the west coast of Mindoro, Apo Reef is a national park, protected for its importance to nesting turtles. Occupying an area of about 15,800ha (57 sq miles), the reef contains three small islets, the largest of which, Apo Island, is surrounded by mangroves.

The reef is also of great interest to divers and underwater photographers as, surrounded by extremely deep waters, it teems with a great diversity of life. Dive safaris are often organized from Puerto Galera during the calm months of April–May, though a much closer access point is the town of Sablayan, on Mindoro's west coast. There is also good diving available here, around **Pandan Island**, a few kilometres offshore.

THE FAR SOUTH

The far south of Luzon, known as **Bicol**, is an intensely volcanic landscape, dominated by the active volcanoes **Mayon** and **Bulusan**.

Legaspi *

Also spelled Legazpi, this port is the largest city in the far south of Luzon. Even so, it is still a small place and one that would have very little interest for the visitor were it not for the huge conical shape of Mt Mayon looming over it. One of the best views can be obtained from the top of **Kapuntukan Hill**, on the coast immediately south of the port.

About 6km (4 miles) northwest of Legaspi are the **Cagsawa Ruins**. Here stands a ruined church, all that remains of a village buried by lava flows following a major eruption in 1814. A further 5km (3 miles) northwest of Cagsawa is Camalig, right at the foot of the volcano, and site of the **Hoyop-Hoyopan Cave**. Though there are various limestone caves in the area, this is the most accessible. A complex of passages filled with stalactites and stalagmites, the cave usually has a cooling wind blowing through its chambers.

There are a number of waterfalls in the area, one of the most accessible being **Busay Falls** near Malilipot, on the northeastern edge of Mt Mayon. This beautiful waterfall has seven levels, with a pool at the base of each leading into the next level below.

Below: *Watching out for the whale sharks of Donsol. The discovery of a resident population has excited marine biologists and triggered both a scramble to ensure their protection and a boom in local tourism.*

Mt Mayon **

At 2421m (7941ft) Mayon is famous not only for being the Philippines' most active volcano, but also for its almost perfect conical shape. The volcano is known to have undergone 44 eruptions, the most recent in 1993, when 70 farmers were killed.

For the non-hiker the closest view of the mountain is from its northern slope: the **Mayon Skyline Hotel** at an altitude of 760m (2500ft). From here there are stunning views of the surrounding countryside and nearby coast.

To climb Mayon, the trail starts on the southern slope from the village of Buyuan. You will need to take all your own equipment and food, and hire a guide. Make arrangements with the Department of Tourism in Legaspi. Remember that the mountain is constantly active and from time to time is closed due to the danger of an eruption.

Above: *Mt Mayon is infamous for its frequent eruptions and the fact that the port city of Legaspi sits rather close to its base.*

Sorsogon **

The two most important attractions of Sorsogon are **Mt Bulusan** and the whale sharks of **Donsol**.

At Donsol, a fishing town 40km (25 miles) south of Legaspi, a whale shark-watching operation has been set up, where visitors can hire a boat and tour the bay to see these gentle giants. Sightings of the fish right at the surface are almost guaranteed, and if you have a mask and snorkel it is possible to swim alongside them. The best time to go is early morning, January–May.

About 80km (50 miles) southeast of Legaspi is Bicol's second active volcano, Mt Bulusan. Surrounded by a 3673ha (9182-acre) national park, many of Bulusan's slopes are cloaked in healthy rain forest, especially in the area around **Bulusan Lake**, a delightful place to explore and one which still has plenty of wildlife. A trail leads up to the summit at 1559m (5114ft) from near the village of San Roque, on the southern side. As for Mayon, you need to take a guide plus all your own food and equipment, and pay attention to eruption warnings. Make arrangements with the provincial tourism council in Sorsogon town.

WHALE SHARKS

This is the world's largest fish, measuring up to 15m (50ft) in length. Being a plankton feeder, however, it is quite harmless. Little is known of its behaviour, but it is thought to be quite rare. Australian researchers normally have to use spotter planes to find any around their coasts, and they count themselves lucky to find 10 in a week. So it came as a big surprise when conservationists discovered a concentration of perhaps as many as 50 in a small area off Donsol. For many years local fishermen had known of them, but it was not until the end of 1997 that the news got out. Now there is a big drive to study their behaviour and ensure that they are protected.

Southern Luzon and Mindoro at a Glance

BEST TIMES TO VISIT

For all parts of this region the driest months are March–May, although Puerto Galera and Legaspi do not have a truly dry season, unlike Calabarzon and western Mindoro. For Puerto Galera and Legaspi the heaviest rain is in November–January, whereas for western Mindoro and Calabarzon this occurs in June–October. Due to rough seas, Apo Reef is generally accessible only in March–May.

GETTING THERE

Regular **bus** services link Manila to many parts of Calabarzon. To reach Puerto Galera, a combined **bus/ferry** ticket can be bought in Manila, with ferries leaving the Centrepoint Hotel in Ermita every morning. The journey takes about five hours. For Sablayan, fly to San José on Mindoro's west coast, and then travel by bus, or take an overnight ferry from Batangas to Sablayan. For Bicol, there are daily **flights** to Legaspi, as well as **buses** and **trains**.

GETTING AROUND

In Calabarzon most of the **bus** services run between Manila and specific points, so getting around from place to place within the region can actually be quite difficult, requiring multiple **jeepney** rides. Self-drive **car hire** from

Manila is an option, made a little difficult by the lack of signposting. In Puerto Galera, most transport is by **boat**, though there are jeepneys in some areas. The west coast of Mindoro has a rough road that is travelled by jeepneys and buses. In Bicol frequent buses link Legaspi with Sorsogon and also the Mt Bulusan area. To get into the Bulusan Volcano National Park, hire a jeepney in Irosin. Donsol is most easily reached by taking a jeepney directly from Legaspi.

WHERE TO STAY

Tagaytay
LUXURY
Taal Vista Hotel, Barangay Kaybagal, Tagaytay City 4120, Cavite, tel: (096) 712-7525, fax: (096) 413-1225. Manila booking office: Room 426, 4th Floor, Makati Stock Exchange Building, Ayala Avenue, Makati City, tel: (02) 817-2710. The best hotel in Tagaytay, situated right on the edge of the Taal caldera, and with spectacular views across the lake and volcano island.

Matabungkay
LUXURY
Coral Beach Club, Matabungkay Beach, Lian, Batangas, tel (cell): 0912 318-4868, fax (cell): 0912 324-3183. A beachfront development, with cottages, a swimming pool and restaurant.

Los Banos
MID-RANGE
City of Springs Resort Hotel, 147 N Villegas St, Los Banos, Laguna, tel: (049) 536-0731, fax: (049) 536-0137. A pleasant hotel in the old part of Los Banos, right on the shores of Laguna de Bay, with a range of room types, a swimming pool, natural spring, and restaurant.

Puerto Galera
MID-RANGE
La Laguna Beach Club, Big La Laguna Beach, Puerto Galera, Oriental Mindoro, tel (cell): 0973 855-545, fax (cell): 0973 878-409, e-mail: lalaguna@epic.net. Manila booking office: Park Hotel, 1032-34 Belen St, Paco, Manila, tel: (02) 521-2371, fax: (02) 521-2393. An attractive beachfront development on Big La Laguna Beach, with its own swimming pool and excellent restaurant.
El Galleon Beach Resort, Small La Laguna Beach, Puerto Galera, Oriental Mindoro, tel (cell): 0973 782-094.

Sablayan
BUDGET
Pandan Island, Pandan Island, 5104 Sablayan, Occidental Mindoro. Manila booking office: Asiaventure, Room 501 Holiday Inn, United Nations Avenue, Ermita, Manila, tel: (02) 526-6929, fax: (02) 523-7007.

Southern Luzon and Mindoro at a Glance

Legaspi

LUXURY

Albay Hotel, 88 Peñaranda St, Legaspi City, Albay, tel: (052) 214-3641, fax: (052) 214-3364. A largish hotel on the northern edge of the city, with views of Mt Mayon.

MID-RANGE

Hotel La Trinidad, Rizal St, Legaspi City, Albay, tel: (052) 480-7335, fax: (052) 214-3148. A city centre hotel with an interesting restaurant.

Casablanca Hotel, Peñaranda St, Legaspi City, Albay, tel: (052) 480-8334, fax: (052) 480-8338. A new hotel near the city centre, with an excellent Chinese restaurant.

Sorsogon

MID-RANGE

Fernandos Hotel, Sorsogon Town, Sorsogon, tel: (056) 211-1537, fax: (056) 211-1537. A new and very pleasant small family-run hotel, with garden and the best restaurant in town. Also the headquarters for the Provincial Tourism Council.

WHERE TO EAT

In most of the places described in this chapter, the best (and often the only) places to eat are in your own hotel or resort. A few additional recommendations are as follows.

Puerto Galera

Puerto Galera Yacht Club, Puerto Galera, Oriental Mindoro, tel: (097) 374-1859.

A terrace restaurant beside Muelle Bay with its own jetty and view of anchored yachts.

Fishermen's Cove, Sto Nino, Puerto Galera, Oriental Mindoro, tel (cell): 0912 306-8494. An Italian restaurant and beach resort close to Puerto Galera.

Relax Thai Restaurant, Sabang, Puerto Galera, Oriental Mindoro, tel (cell): 0973 878781. In the centre of Sabang Village, serves excellent Thai food.

Legaspi

Orient Garden, Casablanca Hotel, Penaranda St, Legaspi City, Albay, tel: (052) 480-8334. An excellent, if slightly expensive, Chinese restaurant inside this new hotel.

TOURS AND EXCURSIONS

Tours of the Calabarzon region can generally be arranged by your Manila hotel. Alternatively, self-drive car hire is easily arranged. In Puerto Galera, to make tours of the coast or to inland areas, make arrangements with your resort. Tours around the Legaspi and Mt Mayon areas can be arranged

with the local office of the Department of Tourism. This office should also be approached for help in organizing a climb up the volcano. Visits to Bulusan Volcano National Park can be arranged through the Sorsogon Provincial Tourism Council.

SPORTS

The main sports are **diving** and **hiking**, the former at Anilao, Puerto Galera, Pandan Island and Apo Reef. The best hiking areas are Taal volcano island, Mt Banahaw, Mt Makiling, Mt Mayon and Mt Bulusan.

USEFUL CONTACTS

Department of Tourism, Region V, Regional Centre Site, Rawis, Legaspi City, Albay, tel: (052) 482-0712, fax: (052) 482-0811.
Sorsogon Provincial Tourism Council, Fernandos Hotel, Sorsogon Town, Sorsogon, tel: (056) 211-1537, fax: (056) 211-1537.
Philippine Airlines, Legaspi Airport Ticket Office, Albay, tel: (052) 445024.

LEGASPI	J	F	M	A	M	J	J	A	S	O	N	D
AVERAGE TEMP. °F	77	79	79	81	82	82	81	82	82	81	81	79
AVERAGE TEMP. °C	25	26	26	27	28	28	27	28	28	27	27	79
RAINFALL ins.	11.8	7	6.4	6.1	6.5	9.9	11.3	10.4	10.6	12.6	18.7	20
RAINFALL mm	301	179	163	155	166	252	287	265	270	320	475	508
DAYS OF RAINFALL	21	15	16	15	14	16	20	18	20	21	22	23

5
Western Visayas

The Visayas form the archipelago that makes up the fractured waist of the Philippines. This is the area where the country's best beaches are situated and where island-hopping is a daily part of life. When people think of the Philippines, it is often specifically the Visayas that spring to mind.

The western Visayas contain the main islands of **Negros** and **Panay**, along with a host of smaller ones that include **Boracay**, home to one of Southeast Asia's most spectacular beaches and the Philippines' number one attraction. Boracay's nearest major town is **Kalibo**, the site each January of **Ati-Atihan**, perhaps the country's most popular festival. At the southern end of Panay is **Iloilo**, an important port and the largest city in the western Visayas. Site of the country's second-oldest Spanish settlement, the surrounding area contains many Spanish churches. The city itself is a working place, but each January – as is the case in Kalibo – the city explodes into festival with **Dinagyang**.

It is a short hop from Iloilo to Negros and its largest city, **Bacolod**. More than half of the country's sugar cane is grown on Negros, and you can see huge estates de-voted to nothing else. Some wild areas have survived, notably **Mt Kanlaon**, the highest mountain in the Visayas, an active volcano surrounded by rain forest. On the east coast, **Dumaguete** is a pleasant university city, with beaches to the south and excellent diving around **Apo Island**. To the north, it is possible to go on whale- and dolphin-watching trips from the town of **Bais**.

DON'T MISS

*** Boracay: a small island lined with dazzling white beaches; also good diving here.
*** Ati-Atihan Festival: held the third weekend of January in Kalibo – a scene of colourful dancing.
** Bais: dolphin- and whale-watching on the Tanon Strait.
** Dumaguete: a pleasant university town, with lovely beaches nearby.

Opposite: *White Beach, several kilometres of white sand, runs along much of the west coast of Boracay, making it one of southeast Asia's island paradises.*

BORACAY

The principal area of interest for the visitor in this region is beautiful Boracay Island. At just 7km (4.5 miles) long and less than 1km (600yd) wide at its narrowest point, this little island is the jewel in the Philippines' crown. The main attraction is **White Beach**, 4km (2.5 miles) of blinding white powdery sand along the west coast, lapped by warm, clear water that in the shallows is enticing aquamarine, changing in the greater depths to a deep cobalt blue.

With three main villages – Manoc-Manoc, Balabag and Yapak – the island has a population of about 6500, though during the height of the visitor season (January–April) numbers swell to way above this. The place has been luring visitors in ever-increasing numbers since the early 1980s, and today some would say Boracay has surpassed saturation point. Small-scale resort developments line virtually the whole of White Beach, and there have been some environmental problems concerning rubbish and sewage, though the locals insist they are getting to grips with this. The north end of the island has recently seen some huge developments, with the creation of a large new golf course and the construction of luxury apartments, something that many people feel has ruined Boracay's simple, rural feeling.

That said, however, Boracay is still a glorious place. Despite the large number of visitors, the beach is big enough to accommodate everyone, ensuring that its relaxed ambience continues. The golf course and the

apartment development remain well out of sight several kilometres away. For those who really do want to get well away from crowds, there are several other lightly used beaches, such as **Diniwid**, just north of White Beach, and **Yapak Beach** at the northern end of the island.

If lazing around on the sand all day is not your kind of thing,

BORACAY'S DIVE SITES

Boracay has plenty of diving facilities, with dive shops scattered along much of the length of White Beach; one of the best is Calypso Diving. Despite dynamite damage to reefs in some areas, Boracay's diving is quite good, and for such a small area remarkably varied. With 12 dive sites immediately around the island itself, and several more further afield, sites vary from coral gardens at a depth of just a few metres (such as Laurel, Crocodile Island and Balinghai Beach) to exciting blue water dives, such as Yapak 1 and 2, which are 35m (115ft) dives onto a ledge where sharks are often seen.

there are plenty of other things to do. On land you can hire bicycles to explore the island, or you could go horse riding. If cycling sounds a bit too energetic, there are plenty of motorized tricycles to be hired – they are the only form of motor transport on the island. On the water, at White Beach there are a number of sailing *bancas* to be hired, outrigger boats that can be very fast and exciting in the right wind, and on the east coast are several **windsurfing** centres.

Inevitably, White Beach is littered with **dive operations**. Boracay's diving is surprisingly good, ranging from coral gardens at reasonably shallow depths to exciting dives into deep blue water where encounters with sharks are quite common.

Above: *A paraw, or sailing outrigger, pulled up onto the beach; Boracay.*
Opposite: *Beach volleyball on Boracay's White Beach.*

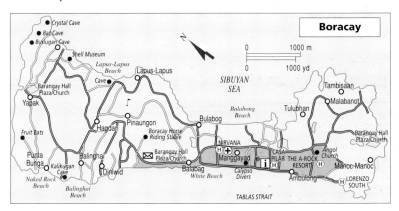

Above: *Drummers at the colourful Ati-Atihan Festival, held each January.*

PANAY

A large, triangular island on the western edge of the Visayas, Panay is a mainly rural area which is divided into four provinces. The eastern half of the island consists of lowlands where several crops, mostly sugar cane and rice, are grown. To the west lies a line of high, partially forested mountains, the tallest of which is Mt Madja-as at 2090m (6855ft).

Kalibo *

Most visitors on their way to or from Boracay pass through Kalibo as this is the destination for the majority of flights between Manila and the region. For most of the year there is little to see in this provincial town. For a couple of weeks each January, however, the town comes alive with its annual festival, **Ati-Atihan**, which culminates on the third weekend of the month in huge dances and parades around town.

The event celebrates agreements struck in the 13th century between the native Aeta people and the immigrating Malays (whose descendants today make up much of Panay's population), who had just crossed from Borneo. In the dances and parades local teams daub their skins black to resemble the early Aeta people and dress in fantastic costumes with intense competition to see which is best. The event is raucous and chaotic, and with zero crowd control this is the ultimate participatory event.

Iloilo *

With a population of around 350,000 Iloilo is Panay's largest city, situated in the south of the island at the mouth of the Iloilo River and sheltered by the island of Guimaras. Today's city sits close to the site of Spain's second Philippine settlement, established in 1566 but moved to the site of the present city in 1700. For many years the area was a major centre for weaving using locally grown Manila hemp and *piña*, the latter a fibre produced from the pineapple leaf. This died away in the second half of the 19th century, though today there has been a small resurgence. Such weaving can be seen in the suburb of **Arevalo**.

Within the city one place worth a visit is the **Museo Iloilo**, where good displays trace much of the city's history and culture (open 09:00–12:00 and 13:00–17:00 daily). For those who enjoy everyday life, the **port** along the south bank of the Iloilo River is worth exploring, as are the two bustling **markets**.

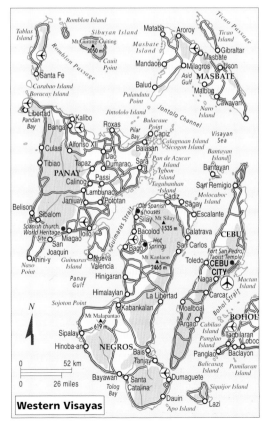

> **SPAIN'S SECOND SETTLEMENT**
>
> After Legaspi established Spain's first Philippine settlement in Cebu in 1565, the threat of a Portuguese attack became very real. It was decided that the Cebu settlement could not be defended and so the Spanish moved to Panay. The exact location is not certain, with sites in both Capiz and Iloilo provinces contending for the title of Spain's second settlement. What is certain is that it was from here that Legaspi launched his attacks on Manila in 1570 and 1571, culminating in the establishment of the new Spanish capital there.

Below: *The Church of Santo Tomas de Villanueva, at Miagao, near Iloilo, Panay, was completed in 1797 and today is a UNESCO World Heritage Site.*

SUGAR CANE

Cultivation of sugar cane began on Negros in the second half of the 19th century, encouraged by Nicholas Loney, British vice consul in Iloilo, to balance his imports of cheap British textiles. Today, about 450,000ha (1700 sq miles) of Negros are given over to sugar cane production, almost all of it on large plantations owned by a few people. Harvest time is from October to April, and this is the time to see the plantations' trains in action, bringing the cane to the sugar mills. The sugar produced on Negros accounts for about 60 per cent of the country's output.

Opposite: *Hikers descend the lower slopes of Mt Kanlaon, where much of the rain forest has been replaced by farmland.*
Below: *The attractive façade of the Negros Occidental Provincial Museum, in Bacolod.*

The suburbs of **Jaro** and **Molo** have attractive Spanish churches, while about 40km (25 miles) to the west **Miagao** has one of the most spectacular. Dating from 1786, this fortress church is a UNESCO World Heritage Site, perhaps due to the superb frieze on the walls above the main entrance, showing a mixture of European figures and tropical vegetation. Still further west the church at **San Joaquin** has a façade recalling the 1859 Spanish–Muslim battle at Tetuan, Morocco.

The main reason to come to Iloilo is to experience the **Dinagyang Festival**, held one week after Kalibo's Ati-Atihan, and similar in style and origins. Another spectacularly colourful event, Iloilo's festival is much more controlled than that of Kalibo, with lavish and highly choreographed dance routines. You have to watch the dancing from a viewing stand.

NEGROS

Negros is a rectangular island, divided along its length by a line of mountains containing six volcanoes, only one of which – Mt Kanlaon – is presently active. The main product is sugar, introduced in the second half of the 19th century. The resulting plantation economy has fostered an immensely wealthy and powerful elite who own the vast sugar *haciendas*. A slump in sugar prices a few years ago caused considerable hardship to the workers, and the island is now attempting to diversify its economy, with increased tourism a major goal.

Bacolod *

Located on the west coast of Negros, Bacolod is the island's largest city. It has little for the visitor, although the **Provincial Museum** has some excellent displays. The city is, however, a good base from which to explore the area. Several **sugar**

plantations can be toured during the cutting season (October–April), and these are especially interesting for their own narrow-gauge railways that bring the sugar cane from the fields to the mills.

To the north of Bacolod the town of **Silay** is known for its old villas, remnants of an era when this was a major port and those who had grown rich on sugar lived here. Inland from the town, you can climb into the hills of **Patag**. There are extensive hiking trails here, and for lovers of beautiful waterfalls it is heaven.

Inland from Bacolod is **Mambucal**, a hot spring resort at the feet of Mt Kanlaon, Negros' only active volcano. The resort is a little rundown, but occupies a lovely spot surrounded by trees, and the baths are hot and relaxing.

Mt Kanlaon **

At 2465m (8085ft) this is the highest mountain in the Visayas and, surrounded by dense rain forest, it is one of the country's most important national parks. On the Bacolod side, trails climb up from Mambucal in the north and the tiny village of **Guintubdan** on the western slopes. A hike from one to the other takes three days.

Make arrangements with the tourism office in Bacolod, where you can pick up guides and porters. Obtain a permit from the national park office in the city, and buy all your supplies before setting off. Take heed of warnings of volcanic activity – Kanlaon last erupted in 1996 and is still active.

A CLIMB UP MT KANLAON

One of the best routes is to start at the little village of Guintubdan and finish at the hot spring resort of Mambucal. At Guintubdan permits are checked, and from here the hike is a steep climb through dense rain forest all the way to the summit. There are two campsites en route: spending the first night at Camp 2 ensures that the summit can be reached within two hours next morning. Just before the summit the forest ends, and there is an old crater, now green and pleasant. At the summit is the active crater, a gaping hole with sheer walls. From the summit to Mambucal is a two-day hike, with a night's camping next to a pretty lake. There is dense forest all the way, and you pass several lakes – the remains of ancient craters. Much of the lower (dipterocarp) forest has been lost, especially around a new geothermal plant. From here it seems to take a long time to reach Mambucal, but when you do the hot spring bath makes it all worthwhile!

Right: *The weekly market at Malatapay, south of Dumaguete, is a colourful and lively affair, well worth visiting for the opportunity it presents to enjoy a slice of rural life.*

At Guintubdan, where permits are checked, you are already in the forest. It is a steep climb for 1½ days to the summit through very dense forest. The summit has a terrifying crater that plunges straight down into the bowels of the earth, and there are stupendous views across Negros to Panay and Cebu. From the summit to Mambucal is a two-day hike passing several lakes that are extinct craters. The last part of the trail passes a new geothermal plant, and after an exhausting climb over a final spur you descend into Mambucal.

Bais **

A pleasant town towards the southern end of the island, Bais is the place to arrange boat trips to watch dolphins and whales frolicking in the nearby **Tanon Strait**, a narrow but incredibly deep stretch of water separating Negros from Cebu. Boats can be arranged through the tourism office. Trips last up to six hours, with sightings virtually guaranteed. You will almost certainly encounter dolphins, since so many live permanently in this part of the strait. Most common are spinner dolphins, but there are also several other species of dolphin, as well as pilot whales and pygmy sperm whales. The really big whales are rarely seen in this confined piece of water.

Dumaguete **

This is an attractive university city on the island's south-east coast. The leafy campus of **Silliman University** takes up a sizeable chunk of the town, while on the

---

CENTROP

The Center for Tropical Conservation Studies was set up in Dumaguete in 1989 to study and conserve the Philippines' native habitats and wildlife. Its headquarters is in an area called the mini-forest in the north of the city, where they have a captive breeding programme for a number of endangered species, including the Philippine spotted deer, the Visayan warty pig and the leopard cat. They also have a captive breeding facility for several species of endangered fruit bat.

northern edge is **Silliman Marine Laboratory**, one of the most important centres for marine biology research in Southeast Asia. Also in the northern part of town is CENTROP, the Center for Tropical Conservation Studies, where a zoo-cum-captive breeding centre keeps a number of endangered mammals that are unique to the Philippines. On the main part of the university campus close to the city centre is an excellent **Anthropology Museum**, with displays of both archaeological finds and the lives of the Philippines' indigenous peoples.

Around Dumaguete **

Looming over Dumaguete is **Cuernos de Negros**, a twin-peaked mountain that is still covered with primary rain forest. One of the peaks, **Mt Talinis**, can be climbed, the trail requiring just a few hours from the roadhead. Make arrangements with the tourist office. Northeast of Talinis is **Lake Balinsasayao**, a beautiful place surrounded by the same rain forest. Access is along a treacherous track that is passable only for four-wheel-drive vehicles.

Along the coast south of Dumaguete are some good beaches, principally at the little town of **Dauin**, 13km (8 miles) to the south of the city. There are a number of pleasant resorts here, which offer diving around nearby **Apo Island**. A marine sanctuary under the protection of the Silliman Marine Laboratory, the reefs around this island are of major importance to conservation. Diving here reveals a huge wealth of coral and fish life, but take great care as the currents can be extremely strong.

About 1000 people live on Apo Island and there is also one resort here. The island can be reached by boat from **Malatapay**, a few kilometres south of Dauin. It is interesting for its Wednesday morning market, a colourful country event of handicrafts, produce and livestock.

> **DIVING AROUND APO ISLAND**
>
> Not to be confused with Apo Reef off the west coast of Mindoro, the reefs around this little island near Dumaguete have been protected by Silliman University's Marine Laboratory since the 1970s. The result is that the reefs here are intact and offer superb diving. Also, being surrounded by deep water, shoals of larger fish such as barracuda, jack and tuna are common. Giant clams and barrel sponges are widespread, along with gorgonian sea fans and a range of hard and soft coral species. Be warned that currents here can be fierce.

Below: *Aboard a dive boat, a diving instructor watches the approach to Apo Island, a popular diving site and an important marine reserve off the southern tip of Negros.*

Western Visayas at a Glance

The rainy season lasts June–December, the dry January–May. The hottest months are April and May. Be in Panay in **January** to catch the Ati-Atihan and Dinagyang festivals. Do not climb any mountains during the rainy season.

Daily **flights** connect Manila to Caticlan (on Panay mainland opposite Boracay), Iloilo, Kalibo and Bacolod. There are also frequent flights to these places from Cebu. Only small planes fly to Caticlan, so most people going to Boracay fly to Kalibo. Special air-conditioned **buses** run from Kalibo airport to the ferry pier at Caticlan. Frequent **bancas** serve as **ferries** between Caticlan and Boracay's White Beach. There is no wharf at White Beach, so you will have to wade ashore.

Ferries run from Manila and Cebu City to Iloilo and Bacolod. A ferry connects Manila with New Washington, which serves Kalibo. Frequent high-speed ferries run between Cebu City and Dumaguete.

On Boracay transportation is by **motorized tricycle** or **bicycle**. Apart from the airport shuttle **buses**, regular **jeepneys** and air-conditioned **minibuses** run between Caticlan and downtown Kalibo. Buses as well as faster and more comfortable minibuses travel between Kalibo and Iloilo. There are several daily high-speed **ferries** between Iloilo and Bacolod.

On Negros, jeepneys link Bacolod with Mambucal and Silay. To reach Guintubdan, take a shuttle bus to La Carlota, then a jeepney. Frequent buses, some air-conditioned, run between Bacolod and Dumaguete. Bus services link Dumaguete with the east coast towns of Malatapay, Dauin and Bais. You will need to hire a vehicle to reach Mt Talinis and Lake Balinsasayao.

Boracay
LUXURY
Nirvana Beach Resort, Balabag, Boracay Island, Aklan, tel: (036) 288-3140, fax: (036) 288-3083. Cottages, five minutes' walk from White Beach.

MID-RANGE
Tonglen Beach Resort, Manggayad, Boracay Island, Aklan, tel: (036) 288-3457, fax: (036) 288-3919. Five minutes' from White Beach; air-conditioned rooms, restaurant.
The A-Rock Resort, Angol, Boracay Island, Aklan, tel: (036) 288-3201, fax: (036) 288-3526. At the southern end of White Beach.

Iloilo
LUXURY
Days Hotel Iloilo, The Atrium at the Capitol, Corner General Luna-Bonifacio Drive, Iloilo City 5000, tel: (033) 337-3297, fax: (033) 336-8000. A brand new hotel built over an indoor shopping mall.

MID-RANGE
Amigo Terrace Hotel, Iznart-Delgado Streets, Iloilo City 5000, tel: (033) 335-0908, fax: (033) 335-0610. A modern, comfortable city hotel.
The Residence, General Luna Street, Iloilo City 5000, tel: (033) 337-2454. A riverside hotel west of the city centre.

Dumaguete
MID-RANGE
Habitat Hotel, Hibbard Avenue, Dumaguete City, tel/fax: (035) 225-2483. New hotel on university campus.
South Sea Resort Hotel, Bantayan, Dumaguete City, tel: (035) 225-2409, fax: (035) 225-0491. North of the city.
El Dorado Beach Resort, Lipayo, Dauin, Dumaguete City, tel: (035) 225-7725, fax: (035) 225-4488. Beachside resort with diving facilities.

Bacolod
LUXURY
Bacolod Convention Plaza Hotel, Magsaysay Avenue, corner Lacson Street, Bacolod City, tel: (034) 835-5158, fax: (034) 433-3757. Modern, air-conditioned, with restaurant.

MID-RANGE
Sugarland Hotel, Araneta Street, Singcang, Bacolod City,

Western Visayas at a Glance

tel: (034) 435-2690, fax: (034) 435-2645. Modern, fully air-conditioned hotel on the main road south out of the city.
Prominence Inn, 158 C Philsugin Road, Bacolod City, tel: (034) 435-0021. Guesthouse with restaurant and garden.

WHERE TO EAT

Boracay
Buffet Restaurant, Manggayad, Boracay Island, Aklan. A fixed-price buffet with superb seafood, meat and vegetables, located just in the southern half of White Beach.
Sulu Tha Thai Restaurant, Angol, Boracay Island, Aklan. Thai food beside White Beach.
English Bakery and Tea Room, English tea, fish and chips, pasties, bacon and eggs, right next to White Beach.

Iloilo
Newbury Street, 2nd Floor, Atrium Mall, General Luna, corner Valeria Streets, Iloilo City 5000. A bar/restaurant, with music, videos and internet.

Dumaguete
Chin Loong, Rizal Boulevard, Dumaguete City, tel: (035) 225-4491. Chinese food.
Opena's, Katada Street, Dumaguete City, tel: (035) 225-0595. A clean self-service restaurant with a wide choice of ready-cooked dishes.

Bacolod
Old West Steak House, Goldenfields Complex, Bacolod

City, tel: (034) 23435. Steaks and other Western cuisine.
Aboy's Kamalig, two branches, tel (Burgos Street): (034) 433-0130, tel (Goldenfields Complex): (034) 435-0760. Filipino cuisine.

TOURS AND EXCURSIONS

On Boracay, there are always boatmen at White Beach for boat tours or snorkelling trips. Agree a price and itinerary before setting off. In Bacolod and Dumaguete, contact the tourist office to arrange transportation and guides for hiking trips. For dolphin and whale-watching trips out of Bais, the municipal tourism office can arrange a boat.

SPORTS

Diving is the main activity, with many dive operators on Boracay. **Windsurfing**, outrigger **sailing** and **cycling** are possible on Boracay. For mountain **hiking** on Negros, contact the tourist offices.

USEFUL CONTACTS

Boracay Tourist Center, Manggayad, Boracay Island, Aklan, tel: (036) 288-3704, fax: (036) 288-3023. An excellent

office providing information, telephone, fax and photo-copying services, ticketing and airline reconfirmation.
Department of Tourism, Bacolod Office, Bacolod Plaza, Bacolod City, tel/fax: (034) 29021, fax: (034) 433-2853.
Department of Tourism, Region VI, Tourism Center, Capitol Ground, Bonifacio Drive, Iloilo City, tel: (033) 337-5411, fax: (033) 335-0245, e-mail: deptour6@iloilo.net.
Tourism Operations Unit, Office of the City Mayor, Bais City 6206, Negros Oriental, tel: (035) 541-5161, fax: (035) 541-5285.
Provincial Tourism Office, Office of the Governor, 2nd Floor, Sidlakang Negros Building, Capitol Area, Dumaguete City, tel: (035) 225-1825.
Calypso Diving, Manggayad, Boracay Island, Aklan, tel: (036) 288-3206, fax: (036) 288-3478.
Philippine Airlines, Kalibo Airport Ticket Office (ATO), tel: (036) 662-3260; Iloilo ATO, tel: (033) 320-3131; Bacolod ATO, tel: (034) 433-3045.

ILOILO	J	F	M	A	M	J	J	A	S	O	N	D
AVERAGE TEMP. °F	79	79	81	84	84	82	81	81	81	82	81	81
AVERAGE TEMP. °C	26	26	27	29	29	28	27	27	27	28	27	27
RAINFALL ins.	1.6	1	1.4	2.2	4.8	12	13.4	14.8	11	10.4	7	3.3
RAINFALL mm	39	26	35	56	121	303	341	375	283	263	177	85
DAYS OF RAINFALL	8	6	5	5	10	19	20	19	19	18	14	11

6
Eastern Visayas

The eastern Visayas consist of Cebu, Bohol, Masbate, Leyte and Samar, the last of these being one of the Philippines' remoter and least visited areas, facing directly onto the Pacific Ocean. **Cebu** and **Bohol** are the two parts of this region best known to visitors – they are home not only to the country's third-largest city but also to some of the best beaches and the finest dive sites. As is the case with the western Visayas, the people here are friendly and getting around presents little problem, with island-hopping an enjoyable part of life.

Cebu City, the capital of Cebu province and site of Spain's first permanent settlement in the Philippines, is the principal gateway. The starting point for many travellers is **Mactan Island**, site of Cebu's airport and a good many luxury resorts. Quite a few small resorts lie along the coast of Cebu, while the main alternative to Mactan is **Moalboal**, a mecca for divers.

Southeast of Cebu lies Bohol, an oval island that has one of the country's best-known landscape features, the **Chocolate Hills**. Off the southwestern coast of Bohol, **Panglao Island** features some of the Visayas' best beaches and diving, the latter concentrating around the tiny island of **Balicasag**.

To the northeast, **Samar** and **Leyte** are still virgin territory for the visitor, with only two well-known sites: **Sohoton National Park**, with its beautiful limestone caves, and **Red Beach** at Palo, the World War II site where General MacArthur landed to drive the Japanese out of the Philippines.

DON'T MISS

*** **Alona Beach:** an attractive beach with excellent diving nearby.
*** **Moalboal:** admittedly only of great interest to divers, but some of the best diving to be had in the Philippines.
** **Chocolate Hills:** strange round hills filling the landscape of central Bohol.
** **Sohoton National Park:** beautiful limestone caves surrounded by forest.

Opposite: *The front of the Basilica Minore del Santo Nino, in Cebu City, home to the Philippines' oldest Christian relic.*

Right: *The Taoist Temple
in the exclusive Beverly
Hills suburb of Cebu City
is a symbol of the wealth
and strength of the local
Chinese community.*

CEBU

Cebu lies at the heart of the Visayas, consisting of a long,
thin island, over 200km (125 miles) long and at most
only 40km (25 miles) wide. Protected to the west by
Negros and to the east by Leyte, and lying south of the
typhoon belt, the area rarely suffers serious storms.
Sadly, almost all of the
island's natural forest has
been destroyed, but along
the coast there are still
numerous small offshore
islands, attractive beaches
and coral reefs.

Cebu City *

The centre of the Visayas
region and capital of Cebu
province, this city of close
to 700,000 people is the
country's third-largest.
Economically it is the
Philippines' second most
powerful city, with the
country's largest port. The
city has been a major trade
centre throughout history.
When Magellan arrived
in 1521 the Chinese had

Cebu City

0	300 m
0	300 yd

Stephenson · Camp. Lapu-Lapu Road · Gaisano · Country Mall

Taoist Temple · A. Villalon Drive · La Guardia · Aznar W. Geonzon Ave · Old Caure Rd · Mactan International Airport

Cebu Country Club
and Golf Course
Sian Tian
Temple

Kamagong · Mojave · Gorodo Ave · Sampaguita · Archbishop Reyes Ave · Pres. Roxas · Ayres Forces Padre · Pres. Magsaysay · Cabahug · E. Labucca · Cebu North Road

Doctors
Hospital · Ayala
Center · P. Cabantan · Juan Luna Ave · North Bus
Terminal

Provincial
Capitol · Ramos Ext · Ma Critina · Luzon Ave · SM Shopping
Mall

V. Rama Ave · J. Avila · **PARK PLACE
HOTEL** · Maxilom Ave · Seventh Ave · Sixth Street · Sixth Ave · Fifth Street · Third Ave · Second Ave

R. Duterte

B. Rodriguez · **CEBU MIDTOWN
HOTEL** · Gen Maxilo Ave

First Street · **DIPLOMAT
HOTEL** · Pres. Osmeña Blvd · **CEBU HARBOR
VIEW HOTEL** · Quezon Blvd Ext.

A. Lopez · Salvador · Pelaez Ext. · D. Jakosalem · T. Padilla

Katipunan · South Bus
Terminal · Skanina · Zulueta

Cebu City
Medical
Center · Cebu Cathedral
Basilica Minore
del Santo Niño · Department of
Tourism · **N**

N. Bacaiso Ave · C. Padilla · Carbon Public
Market · Tupas · Magellan's
Cross · M.C. Briones · City Hall

Spolarium · Quezon Blvd. · Fort San Pedro

already been here for centuries. It was not until 1565 that the Spanish came to stay, **Miguel Lopez de Legaspi** establishing Spain's first permanent settlement here.

Today, the city is expanding all the time, reaching out onto areas reclaimed from the sea. Inland, the suburbs climb up into the foothills of the central mountain range, culminating in several locations with views of the city and cool night-time temperatures.

The city itself clearly falls into old and new parts. The former, crowded and a bit down at heel, includes some of the shopping areas, including **Colon Street**, the oldest street in the Philippines and site of Legaspi's first settlement. The newer part, bustling but cleaner, spacious and clearly wealthier, is further north around Fuente Osmeña, Maxilom Avenue and the Ayala Center, the latter being a major indoor shopping centre.

Many places of interest lie in the old area, starting with the **Basilica Minore del Santo Nino** – a church that houses Cebu's most important Christian relic, a small statue of the infant Jesus that was given by Magellan in 1521 to Queen Juana, wife of Raha Humabon, the local chieftain. This basilica is the focus of Cebu's main festival, **Sinulog**, held in the third week of January.

Close to the basilica, housed in a small chapel, is **Magellan's Cross**, a replica of one planted here by Magellan when the very first Filipinos were baptized. To the southeast on the waterfront stands **Fort San Pedro**, built by the Spanish to ward off pirate attacks. Further north is the **Casa Gorordo Museum**, originally the home of Cebu's first Filipino bishop. The old house is furnished and decorated in the style of the wealthy of the late Spanish era.

In the affluent suburb of Beverly Hills, a testament to the strength of the local Chinese community, is an enormous **Taoist Temple**, well worth a visit for its insight into the Chinese Filipino world. Further out of town from here is **Tops**, a hilltop viewpoint that has spectacular views of the city below.

MAGELLAN IN CEBU

When Ferdinand Magellan arrived in Cebu on 7 April 1521 he opened a new chapter in Philippine history. **Raha Humabon**, the local chief, was remarkably receptive to Magellan, and after making a blood pact he agreed to be baptized. This, the first baptism in the Philippines, took place on Sunday 14 April 1521. It was probably to demonstrate his fighting skills that Magellan took on Humabon's neighbour, **Lapu-Lapu**, chief of Mactan Island. On 27 April, 48 Spaniards took on 1500 of Lapu-Lapu's warriors, a clash that Magellan did not survive.

Below: *Magellan's Cross is a replica of one that Ferdinand Magellan set up after his arrival in 1521.*

Opposite: Climbing into a tricycle, the only transport available between Panagsama Beach and the nearby town of Moalboal.
Below: *Shangri-La's Mactan Island Resort is probably the largest and most spectacular of the resorts strung out along the east coast of the island.*

THE WORLD'S MOST ENDANGERED BIRD?

In a country where much of the wildlife is dependent on healthy rain forest it is not surprising to hear that in Cebu, where virtually all the forest has been cleared, wildlife has suffered badly. One such example is the **Cebu flowerpecker**, a tiny, pretty bird that feeds on the nectar of certain forest flowers, and which is absolutely unique to Cebu. Some years ago it was thought extinct, but in 1991 was re-discovered in a tiny patch of forest in the island's central mountains. Today it hangs onto survival by a thin thread, its total world population just four individuals.

Mactan Island **

To the east of Cebu City lies Mactan Island, site of Cebu's international airport. Also here is Cebu's main tourist belt – Mactan's east coast is lined with resorts, many of them luxury developments catering to tourists from all over the world. Most of the resorts are concentrated along the intermittent beaches.

At the northern end of the island, near Punta Engaño, are two **monuments**, one to **Magellan** and the other to **Lapu-Lapu**, the local chieftain who killed Magellan on this spot in April 1521. Further south, at Maribago, are workshops dedicated to making one of Cebu's most famous traditional products – **guitars**. Visitors can buy them here, and also watch the manufacturing process.

Off Mactan's east coast lies another, quite different island – **Olango**. Though the northern half of this low-lying island is populated, with two villages, the southern half consists of a vast expanse of mangroves and mud-flats that during the winter months are home to tens of thousands of migratory birds. Now a nature reserve, this is an ideal place for birdwatchers. The island is easily reached by ferry from Maribago.

Moalboal **

Approximately 90km (60 miles) from Cebu City and easily reached by bus, this small, friendly town has for some years been attracting divers in large numbers. The

centre of action for visitors is **Panagsama Beach**, situated about 3km (2 miles) from the town. Here, a rather untidy jumble of restaurants, guesthouses and dive operations straggles along a shore that in itself is rather disappointing for the beach lover. All the sand along this shore was swept away by a typhoon in 1984, leaving the nearest sandy beach a 15-minute boat ride to the north, at the appropriately named **White Beach**.

That Moalboal nevertheless continues to attract visitors can probably be attributed to its superb diving. Although the coral reef immediately in front of the beach was also destroyed by the 1984 typhoon (and today is slowly regenerating), other areas nearby remained intact and currently represent some of the best diving in the Visayas. The main point of interest is **Pescador Island**, a tiny slab of rock a couple of kilometres offshore and about 15 minutes by boat to the south of Panagsama Beach. The island, a marine reserve that has been extremely well protected, is the pinnacle of a submarine mountain, surrounded by a coral reef that slopes gently for a short distance before plunging off in a vertical wall into the depths of the sea. The reef top has an enormous diversity of corals, while both here and on the wall there is an abundance of marine life. A similar reef can be seen off **Tongo Point**, which is situated on the mainland about 1km (0.6 mile) south of Panagsama Beach.

Moalboal is also increasingly being used as a base to explore some of the inland areas. Hiking and mountain biking tours can be arranged at Panagsama Beach, and it is possible to make a trip to **Kawasan Falls**, an attractive place surrounded by forest vegetation, approximately 20km (12.5 miles) to the south.

MOALBOAL DIVE SITES

Most diving here concentrates on **Pescador**, a tiny island that is the summit of a submerged mountain lying a couple of kilometres offshore. The island is ringed by a coral ledge at a depth of 3–9m (10–30ft) which becomes a sheer wall dropping to a depth of 30–50m (100–165ft). The ledge is covered with a huge wealth of corals in pristine condition, while the wall is covered in gorgonian sea fans, sponges, cup corals and many other corals. Fish life is abundant. On the western side is the 'Cathedral', an open-top funnel. A number of sites along the shore of the mainland, such as **Tongo Point**, also have reefs in excellent condition with extensive fish life.

Above: *The Loboc River, one of the main rivers draining Bohol, makes its way slowly through an intensely green landscape in the south of the island.*

BOHOL

To the east of Cebu lies Bohol, tenth-largest of the Philippine islands and for the visitor one of the most attractive. The coast, with its beaches and coral reefs, is what draws most visitors, while inland lie the **Chocolate Hills**, one of the country's best-known and unique landscapes.

Historical interest lies in the large number of old Spanish churches that dot the landscape, some of the first to be built anywhere in the Philippines. They stem from a 16th-century blood pact between Legaspi and local leader Raha Sikatuna. These churches have survived despite Bohol being the scene of one of the few truly successful Filipino uprisings against the Spanish, which saw the island manage to maintain independence for 86 years (1744–1829).

Tagbilaran and Area **

Tagbilaran, situated in the southwest of the island, is the capital of Bohol. It has little of interest for the visitor, though an exploration of the surrounding countryside is worthwhile. On the eastern edge of town, at **Bool**, is a memorial to the Sikatuna–Legaspi pact, while about 7km (4.5 miles) east of town is **Baclayon**, site of the Church of the Immaculate Conception, the oldest stone church in Bohol, built in 1727. Approximately 15km (10 miles) east of Tagbilaran is the town of **Loay**, the place where the River Loboc runs into the sea. From here, head inland to the village of **Loboc**, a pleasant little place on the banks of the river of the same name. This is the site of another old church, the Church of San Pedro, built a few years after the one at Baclayon. It is possible to hire boats here for trips up the river.

About 35km (20 miles) north of Tagbilaran the town of **Antequera** is known for its Sunday morning market, a place to buy many of the area's handicrafts, particularly basketry. Just 1km (0.6 miles) from town are the **Mag-Aso Falls**, one of the loveliest waterfalls in Bohol.

Chocolate Hills **

This strange landscape of hundreds of small rounded hills, 50–120m (165–400ft) high, lies in the middle of Bohol about 50km (30 miles) northeast of Tagbilaran, and is rated as one of the most important visitor landmarks in the country. It seems to be absolutely unique not just to the Philippines but actually to Bohol. Although for most of the year the hills are green with grass, by the end of the dry season, in April or May, much of it has died and turned brown, giving these hills their name.

The nearest town is **Carmen**, situated at the edge of Chocolate Hills and easily accessible from Tagbilaran. Any part of the hills can be explored, but life has been made easy by the establishment of a viewpoint on the summit of one of the largest, thus ensuring an all-round view of the landscape. The hills are said to be especially beautiful at dusk and dawn, the viewing of which entails an overnight stay in the area's limited accommodation.

> **MAKING THE CHOCOLATE HILLS**
>
> Geologists believe that the strange Chocolate Hills were created by weathering of coralline limestone lying above heavy clay. As ever, mythology has a far more colourful explanation, claiming that the hills are the debris left after a fight between two giants. The giants apparently threw rocks at each other for several days until both were quite worn out. Making friends, they left the scene of the battle, with the newly formed hills as evidence of the fight.

Below: *The Chocolate Hills are a landscape feature utterly unique to this one island, and are one of the Philippines' most famous sights.*

Opposite: *Balicasag Island, site of an important marine reserve and one of the Philippines' best dive sites.*
Below: *Alona Beach, Bohol's main coastal resort. Situated on the southern shore of Panglao Island, it offers a more intimate alternative to Boracay.*

Panglao Island ★★★

Off the southwest coast of Bohol, the island of Panglao is home to Bohol's best beaches, most notably **Alona Beach**. Here plenty of accommodation has been built among coconut groves along the edge of a stunningly beautiful white beach. Alona represents a quieter and less crowded alternative to Boracay.

Alona is good not just for the sun lover but also for the diver. Panglao is surrounded by excellent dive sites, starting with the house reef a short distance off the beach. About 9km (6 miles) to the southwest is tiny **Balicasag Island**, like Pescador Island a marine reserve with some of the country's best diving. Dive trips run daily from Alona Beach to Balicasag, or you can stay on the island. Although Balicasag has a shallow sloping coral garden, it is known mostly for its walls, where the island plunges into the depths of the sea. Here are plenty of corals and abundant fish life, including large shoals of jack, barracuda and sometimes tuna.

Other Islands ★★

About 11km (7 miles) off the coast from Baclayon and one hour south by boat from Alona Beach lies **Pamilacan Island**, the site of a community of fishing people who specialize in catching whales, sharks and manta rays. Though catching all these animals has recently become illegal, they continue the business as their only source of income. The waters around this island seem to be one of the main areas in the whole of the Philippines for whales and dolphins, and the World Wide Fund for Nature (WWF) is presently working with the local people to set up whale-watching trips as a sustainable livelihood. There is no accommodation on Pamilacan Island, but such trips can be arranged in Tagbilaran or upon arrival on Pamilacan. The island can be reached by boat from Baclayon.

On the west coast of Bohol, 30km (20 miles) northwest of Tagbilaran, **Cabilao Island** is surrounded by a marine reserve known for its superb coral formations. There is accommodation, and the island can be reached from Loon on the Bohol mainland. Alternatively, dive operators in Cebu and Panglao Island often run dive trips to Cabilao.

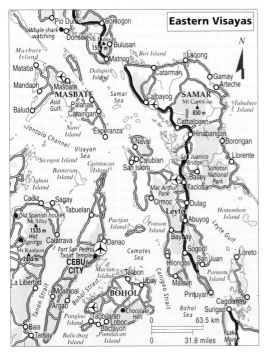

PANGLAO DIVE SITES

The dive sites here offer virtually every kind of diving available in the Philippines. On the northern side of Panglao Island are Napaling and Duljo, the first a beautiful, sloping coral garden with a wall, the latter a deep dive along a wall that drops to 40m (130ft). The most famous dive sites are those around nearby **Balicasag Island**, where walls and coral gardens are home to table corals, gorgonian sea fans, sponges, and large shoals of pelagic fish such as barracuda, jacks, snappers and batfish. There is also a wealth of reef fish, such as moorish idols, damselfish and butterflyfish.

DESTRUCTIVE FISHING

Much damage has been done to coral reefs in the past by two very destructive fishing methods: the use of **dynamite** and **cyanide**. The latter is used to catch reef fish for the aquarium trade. A small amount squirted in a crevasse on a reef stuns the fish, but kills the nearby corals. Dynamite fishing over a reef kills or stuns fish, which float to the surface, and devastates large parts of the reef. With the coral dead, fish stocks rapidly decline. Only when the reef recovers, so will fish life. Both methods are illegal, but until recently enforcement has been lax. Protection has improved in most areas and many reefs are starting to recover.

Right: *The Leyte Landing
Memorial at MacArthur
Park recalls the famous
scene of General Douglas
MacArthur walking ashore
after the successful
American landings in 1944.*
Below: *One of the
Stations of the Cross, on a
hill overlooking Tacloban.*

SAMAR AND LEYTE

These two large islands, separated by a narrow strip of
water spanned by the San Juanico Bridge, form the
easternmost edge of the Visayas, protecting this central
part of the Philippines from the force of the Pacific
Ocean. Both islands remain largely unexplored by
visitors, are relatively thinly populated and still have
some extensive areas of forest. Leyte, especially, has volcanic activity, with many hot springs that are now being
tapped for geothermal energy.

Tacloban and Area *

Tacloban, the capital of Leyte, has little of interest to the
visitor, though its setting is attractive – on a small bay
completely enclosed by the long sweeping arm of Samar
to the east. There is a great view from the hill above
town, on which stands a statue of Christ.

A HOWLING WILDERNESS

The American takeover of the
Philippines was not without
some brutality. The most
famous incident occurred in
Samar in 1901–2. A Filipino
uprising in the town of
Balangiga resulted in the
deaths of many of the
American soldiers stationed
there. The reprisals were
swift and extreme. General
'Jake' Smith, organizing the
pacification of Samar,
ordered that anyone capable
of carrying arms, even 10-
year-old children, were to be
killed so that Samar could be
turned into 'a howling wilderness'. Six months and many
massacres later, he had succeeded. Smith was eventually
court-martialled.

About 10km (6 miles) south of Tacloban at the town of **Palo** is **Red Beach** and **MacArthur Park**, where American troops first landed in 1944 to retake the Philippines from the Japanese. Centrepiece of the park is a dramatic memorial showing the famous scene of MacArthur and his commanders wading ashore. In Palo there is an old cathedral, while close by is **Hill 522**, scene of intense fighting between American and Japanese troops. Today, the hill has an attractive and peaceful view over the town and coast.

Sohoton National Park **

Known for its deep ravines, limestone scenery and caves, this 840ha (2100-acre) national park, though situated on Samar, is most easily reached from Tacloban as a day trip. You first make for the village of Basey, where you obtain a permit and guide, and then travel for an hour by boat upriver, before entering the forest and a limestone gorge. Soon, the boat pulls up to a landing hemmed in by cliffs, and from here the guide and a ranger guide you through the most accessible cave, called Panhulugan I. Well protected by its isolation, it is still in pristine condition, with all its stalactites and stalagmites intact and free of graffiti. There are no artificial structures – all is as nature created it – and the result is stunningly beautiful.

From here it is possible to hike a little in the forest and then to continue upriver by boat, but only if the water level is high enough. Some way upriver from the cave a **natural stone bridge** spans the river gorge from one cliff face to the other, there are more caves, and at the furthest point of the park, well beyond the reach of any boat and necessitating a hike through the forest, are the 80m-high (260ft) **Cabungaan Falls**.

Below: *Panhulugan I Cave, Sohoton National Park, Samar.*

Eastern Visayas at a Glance

BEST TIMES TO VISIT

Cebu has no distinct dry season, though February–May
are the driest. April and May
are the hottest months. Bohol
is similar, though rains usually
arrive only in August. Samar
and Leyte have no distinct dry
season, but their rainiest period
is November–January.

GETTING THERE

Cebu has the country's second-
largest international airport,
with **flights** direct from Hong
Kong, Japan, Malaysia and
Singapore. There are many
daily flights between Cebu
and Manila. Tacloban is also
linked to Manila by regular
flights. There are frequent
flights into Cebu from most
major Philippine cities. Regular
ferries link Manila with the
region. High-speed ferries link
Tagbilaran and Cebu with
Mindanao and Negros; slow
ferries connect Cebu to most
areas in the country.

GETTING AROUND

There are **flights** several times
a week between Cebu and
Tacloban; other inter-island
transport is by **ferry**. Slow
ferries link most islands, while
fast, comfortable **catamarans**
cover main routes. Regular
fast ferries run from Cebu to
Ormoc, from where there are
bus connections to Tacloban.
Several fast ferries run
between Cebu and Tagbilaran.
Within Cebu, the island is
served by **buses**, some

air-conditioned. In Bohol, buses
are small and battered, rather
like the roads. There are also
jeepneys. In Samar and Leyte
buses and air-conditioned
minibuses ply the route from
the ferry pier at Ormoc to Tacloban, and there are jeepneys
between Tacloban and Palo.
There is only an infrequent
jeepney service to Basey.
Chauffeur-driven **cars** can be
hired in Cebu City, Tagbilaran
and Tacloban, but self-drive
cars only in Cebu City. Within
Cebu City metered **taxis** are
plentiful; for a journey from
the city to Mactan Island drivers
usually don't use the meter. For
a fee they will also take you
anywhere in Cebu province.
In Tagbilaran and Tacloban,
taxis are infrequent; most
local transportation is by
tricycle.

WHERE TO STAY

Cebu City
LUXURY
Cebu Midtown Hotel, Fuente
Osmeña, Cebu City, tel: (032)
253-9711, fax: (032) 253-9765.
Overlooks Osmeña Circle.

MID-RANGE
Kan-Irag Hotel, F. Ramos St,
Cebu City, tel: (032) 253-
1151, fax: (032) 253-6935.
An old building, huge rooms.

Mactan Island
LUXURY
**Shangri-La's Mactan Island
Resort**, Punta Engaño Road,
PO Box 86, Lapu-Lapu City

6015, Cebu, tel: (032) 231-
0288, fax: 231-1688.
Comfortable rooms, two
pools, lush gardens, a beach
with boats to hire, hotel's
own dive operation, several
restaurants.

MID-RANGE
Tambuli Beach Club,
Buyong, Mactan Island, Cebu;
c/o 16 Borromeo Arcade, F
Ramos Street, Cebu City, tel:
(032) 52855, fax: (032) 53097.
A beachside resort with four
pools and a lush garden.

Moalboal
MID-RANGE
Cabana Beach Club Resort,
Panagsama Beach, Moalboal,
Cebu, tel/fax: (032) 253-7661.
Cottages on the beach.

BUDGET
Marina Beach Resort,
Panagsama Beach, Moalboal,
Cebu, tel/fax: (032) 340-9935,
tel (cell): 0918 770-7817.
Bungalows near the beach.

Alona Beach and Balicasag Island
MID-RANGE
**Balicasag Island Dive
Resort**, Balicasag Island, Bohol.
Manila booking address:
Ground Floor, Glass Exchange
Corner Building, 107 Herrera
Street, Legaspi Village, Makati
City, tel: (02) 810-4504, fax:
(02) 812-1164.

BUDGET
Alona Tropical, Alona Beach,

Eastern Visayas at a Glance

Panglao Island, Bohol, tel (cell): 0918 740-1668, fax: (028) 175-410.

Tacloban
LUXURY
Leyte Park, Magsaysay Blvd, Tacloban, Leyte, tel: (053) 325-6000, fax: (053) 325-5587. Near the sea and city centre.

MID-RANGE
MacArthur Park Beach Resort, Government Center, Palo, Tacloban, Leyte, tel: (053) 323-3015. Large complex laid out in gardens, next to Red Beach and MacArthur Park.

WHERE TO EAT

Cebu City has many restaurants; elsewhere you would eat at your hotel or resort.

Cebu City
Swiss Chalet Restaurant, Babag 1, Cebu City 6000, tel/fax: (032) 412-6305. A Swiss restaurant situated at a cool altitude of 600m (2000ft), on hills overlooking the city.
Ang Lasang Singapura, Level 3, Ayala Center, Cebu, tel: (032) 232-6142. A Singaporean restaurant inside huge indoor shopping centre.
Lantaw Gardens, Plaza Club, Cebu Plaza Hotel, Nivel Hills, Lahug, Cebu City, tel: (032) 231-1231. A hotel restaurant serving Filipino food in the cool elevation of the hills above the city. Cultural presentations on Friday and Saturday evenings.

Golden Cowrie, Cor Salinas Drive, La Guardia, Lahug, tel: (032) 92633. An inexpensive Filipino seafood restaurant.

SHOPPING

In Cebu City the downtown shopping district is rather chaotic. Carbon Market is good for Philippine **handicrafts**, particularly **basketry**. For air-conditioned comfort head to the SM Mall or Ayala Center, a huge indoor mall with shops that sell just about everything, including handicrafts. On Mactan Island, there are numerous **guitar** factories.

TOURS AND EXCURSIONS

The luxury hotels on Mactan Island can arrange tours for their guests, while in Cebu City the tourist office, travel agents and car hire companies can help. On Alona Beach, ask your guesthouse to arrange car, tricycle or motorbike hire. In Tacloban the tourist office will help arrange a trip to Sohoton National Park.

SPORTS

The main sport is **diving**, with dive operations available at the main resorts. **Windsurfing** is

also available at some of the Mactan Island resorts. In Moalboal **mountain biking** and **hiking** trips can be arranged.

USEFUL CONTACTS

Department of Tourism, Region VII, Ground Floor, LDM Building, Lapu-Lapu Street, Cebu City, tel: (032) 254-2811, fax: 254-2711.
Department of Tourism, Region VIII, Children's Park, Sen. Enage St, Tacloban City, tel: (053) 321-2048, fax: (053) 325-5279.
Savedra Dive Center, Panagsama Beach, 6032 Moalboal, tel/fax: (032) 340-9935, e-mail: 7seas@infocen.com.ph.
Genesis Divers, Alona Beach, 6340, Panglao Island, Bohol, tel: 0918 770-8434, fax: 0912 516-6075, e-mail: genesis@cebu.webling.com.
Planet Action, Panagsama Beach, 6032 Moalboal, tel (cell): 0918 770-8686, e-mail: CebuAcc@ibm.net. Mountain biking and hiking trips.
Philippine Airlines, Cebu, reservations and enquiries tel: (032) 340-0191; Tacloban Airport Ticket Office, tel: (053) 325-6960.

CEBU	J	F	M	A	M	J	J	A	S	O	N	D
AVERAGE TEMP. °F	80	81	82	84	84	83	83	83	83	82	82	81
AVERAGE TEMP. °C	26	27	28	29	29	28	28	28	28	28	28	27
RAINFALL ins.	4.2	3	2.2	1.8	2.8	7.5	7.6	6	7	7.2	5.8	5
RAINFALL mm	104	75	54	44	71	188	192	148	174	182	148	127
DAYS OF RAINFALL	11	8	7	5	6	14	15	12	14	15	12	12

7
Mindanao and Sulu

Recognized as the home of most of the Philippines' Muslims, sadly until recently parts of Mindanao and the Sulu Islands were off most visitors' travel itineraries due to a plague of communist and Islamic separatist guerrilla groups. Since the early 1990s, however, the main warring factions have signed treaties with the government and most of the south is now peaceful. Only a couple of small guerrilla groups remain active, leaving just a few pockets off-limits.

One of the advantages of all this past violence is that larger tracts of intact wilderness, especially forest, have survived here than in most other parts of the country. For the energetic, hiking trails are being developed in some of the mountain areas, the most challenging climb being up **Mt Apo**, the Philippines' highest mountain.

Beaches are less well developed here than in the Visayas, but **Samal Island**, close to the city of **Davao**, is now being promoted as a resort. At the northern end of Mindanao, **Camiguin Island** is already thought of as something of a tropical paradise, especially by urban Filipinos, mainly for its very friendly people and beautiful, lush scenery, complete with a climbable active volcano. In the northeast, **Siargao Island** has become the latest mecca for surfers.

To the southwest stretch the **Sulu Islands**, a long and scattered chain reaching out towards Borneo. Island-hopping here takes you through some of the Philippines' main Muslim areas, with a culture utterly different from most of this predominantly Christian country.

TOP ATTRACTIONS

*** Camiguin Island: lovely scenery and friendly people.
** Siargao Island: surfing, fine beaches, great scenery.
** Mt Apo: the highest mountain in the Philippines, surrounded by dense forest.
** Philippine Eagle Nature Center: breeding centre for endangered Philippine eagles and other wildlife.
* Fort del Pilar: home to the Marine Life Museum.
* Climaco Freedom Park: a hillside park with views across Zamboanga.
* Sitangkai: a town built on stilts over a coral reef.

Opposite: *A banca on the shore of Daco, an islet offshore from Siargao Island.*

Below: *Vast pineapple plantations spread across large areas of northern Mindanao, especially in Bukidnon province to the south of Cagayan de Oro. In the distance is the Mt Kitanglad range, an important national park.*

NORTHERN MINDANAO

This region stretches from the university city of **Cagayan de Oro** in the west through **Butuan** to **Surigao** in the far north. Close to Surigao is a series of **caves**, while off the coast lies **Siargao Island**. To the southwest, Butuan is possibly one of the oldest settlements in the Philippines: prehistoric human remains have been found here, as has a large 1000-year-old ocean-going outrigger, a **balangay**, now housed in its own museum.

Inland from Cagayan de Oro one climbs into the mountains of **Bukidnon** province. Here are vast pineapple plantations, as well as the **Mt Kitanglad** range, its rain forest a known stronghold of the endangered Philippine eagle. A hiking trail leads up to Dulang-Dulang, at 2938m (9637ft) the highest peak in the range and also the second-highest mountain in the Philippines.

Off the coast between Cagayan de Oro and Butuan lies **Camiguin Island**, one of the most beautiful jewels of the entire country.

Camiguin Island ★★★

This mountainous, 300km² (108 sq mile) island is perhaps Mindanao's most beloved attraction. With no less than five volcanoes crammed into it, Camiguin's steep mountain slopes rise to a height of 1713m (5619ft) at Mt Mambajao, the tallest of the volcanoes. Only one of the volcanoes is presently active and that is **Hibok-Hibok**, which last erupted in 1951.

The capital of Camiguin Island is the little town of **Mambajao**. The main local activities are fishing and farming, making use of the rich volcanic soil and the nearby deep-sea trenches. The people are extremely relaxed and friendly.

Beaches line much of the island's coast, though the sands are a volcanic grey. The coast is beautiful, nevertheless, made all the more so by its stupendous mountain backdrop. There is some reasonable diving here, principally on the coral reef off nearby **Mantigue Island**, on the intermittent corals around **White Island**, just offshore from **Agoho**, on

Camiguin's northern tip, and also on the submarine slopes of **Mt Vulcan Daan**, which is one of the island's volcanoes.

Inland there are several waterfalls, as well as hot and cold springs. Close to the northern end of the island **Katibawasan Falls** is a spectacular ribbon of water plunging vertically 50m (165ft) into a pool, while not far away is **Ardent Hot Springs**. You can soak in a hot pool here, or if you are feeling energetic you can hike to the summit of Hibok-Hibok, a climb that takes about four hours from the hot spring starting point.

Above: *A fishing family enjoying the last rays of the setting sun on the beach at Agoho, Camiguin Island.*

BUTUAN

Today Butuan is a rather unremarkable city that has little to attract the visitor. Yet 1000 years ago it was the trading hub of the Philippines, possibly an eastern outpost of Srivijaya, a Southeast Asian empire, and a place that had extensive contacts with China. Large finds of ancient Chinese pottery and coins have been made in Butuan, while the city is mentioned in Chinese annals of the Song and Yuan dynasties (10th–14th century). Remains of two large ocean-going vessels have been found in Butuan, one of which has been moved to Manila's National Museum.

Mindanao & Sulu

0   100 km
0   50 miles

SULU SEA

Binalbagan
Canayan
Hinoba-an
Bayawan
Dapitan
Siquijor Island
Camiguin Island
Sindangan
Dipolog
Datagan
Siocon
Sibuco
Zamboanga
Fort del Pilar
Isabela
Basilan Island
Jolo

Tawi-Tawi Island
Bongao
Sitangkai

Argao
Tagbilaran
Bohol Island
Mt Hibok-Hibok ▲1320 m
Butuan
Museum
Iligan
Mt Dulang Dulang ▲2938 m
Lake Lanao
Pagadian
Kidapawan
Mt Apo ▲2954 m
Tacurong
General Santos
Glan

Siargao Island
Surigao
Cloud Nine
Tandag
Cagayan de Oro
Malaybalay
DAVAO
Tagum
Samal Island
Bobon
Balut Island
Sarangani Island

CELEBES SEA

N

Above: *Navigating a boat through the shallow reef that surrounds Guyam, a tiny islet close to Siargao Island.*

Siargao Island ★★

Off the northernmost tip of Mindanao lies Siargao Island, or rather group of islands and islets. The entire island group is a protected area, due to its varied habitats, which include fragments of lowland rain forest, the country's largest mangrove swamp, beautiful coastal views and an undamaged coral reef.

A growing flow of foreign visitors has been coming to Siargao since the mid-1990s, but not because of its conservation value. This is a new surf mecca. Surf breaks occur right up and down the island's east coast, though the most famous is **Cloud Nine**, just north of the town of **General Luna** (usually known simply as GL). Three-metre (9ft) waves surge in straight from the Pacific Ocean, rolling up to form almost perfect tubes before breaking on the coral reef below. The surf is best from June to November, during the typhoon season. This area is actually south of the typhoon belt and so is rarely hit by storms, but it does get the ocean swell from typhoons passing to the north.

For the non-surfer there are a number of attractions. There is quite a nice beach at GL, though the best are on some of the outer islands. **Guyam Islet**, for example, is little more than a sand bar with a few coconut palms on it, but is ringed by a white beach and has excellent snorkelling over a shallow coral reef nearby. There is another superb beach on **Daco Island**, a little further out from Guyam.

On **Bucas Grande Island**, to the southwest of Siargao but still part of the protected area, is **Suhoton Cave**, while at **Del Carmen** on the western side of Siargao boats can be hired to tour the mangroves. There are crocodiles in this swamp.

CAMIGUIN MYTHOLOGY

According to mythology Camiguin was formed as a result of the love between a princess of northern Mindanao and a visiting warrior from the Visayas. They were forbidden to marry, but as he sailed away she attempted to swim after the boat. Sadly she drowned, but the gods took pity on her, raising her body back above the surface. Although they could not restore her to life, they could transform her into any form they wished, and so she became a paradise island and Camiguin was born. To this day, her love for the Visayan warrior remains so strong that every now and then she erupts into fiery displays of passion – the fireworks of Camiguin's volcanoes.

SOUTHERN MINDANAO

The main urban area here is Davao, one of the country's largest cities, which with the return of peace to Mindanao is now enjoying a boom. In the countryside, the landscape varies from low-lying marshland and grassy plains to the country's highest mountain, and vegetation from rice fields and plantations to dense forest. Much of the plantation farming consists of the ubiquitous coconut and banana, but you will also find the banana-like plant **abaca**, the fibres of which are spun into Manila hemp. **Durian**, the large spiny fruit that smells like a sewer and supposedly tastes like heaven, is also grown extensively in the region, its large solid trees giving the impression of forest. When in season its smell permeates even the streets of Davao, and it is no coincidence that the city is sometimes known as the durian capital of the Philippines.

Davao *

With a land area of 2440km² (880 sq miles), Davao is officially the Philippines' largest city. Most of the municipal region is open countryside and even forested mountain, however, the city itself occupying a relatively small area on the coast. Still, with a population of 900,000 it is certainly the country's second most populous city. There is little of interest within the urban area of Davao, except for the **Fuentespina Orchid Garden**, a marvellous place for lovers of flowers, and a good opportunity to see the Waling-waling, a beautiful pink or peach-coloured orchid that is Davao's emblem.

SULTAN KUDARAT

When the Spanish started to establish themselves in the Philippines they discovered that Islam had been arriving from the south. The Bruneian ruler of Manila, for example, had become a Muslim only a few years before Legaspi's arrival. Islam quickly lost ground to the Spanish in most of the country, but strongly resisted the Christian invasion in Mindanao and Sulu. In the 17th century the Spanish were repeatedly defeated by Sultan Kudarat, head of the Maguindanao Sultanate and great-great-grandson of Kabungsawan, founder of Mindanao's first Islamic sultanate.

Below: *Surfing Cloud Nine on a relatively calm day. Siargao Island, especially Cloud Nine, is the latest surf hotspot due to its reliable and usually huge surf breaks.*

Below: *Traffic in Davao,
largest city in Mindanao.*

To the south of the city is the **Shrine of the Holy
Infant Jesus of Prague**, set in a pleasant park and
located on a hill with a good view of the city. At Lanang,
on the northern side of the city, next to the Insular
Century Hotel Davao is the **Davao Museum**, housing a
display of artefacts belonging to some of the many tribal
groups that live in Mindanao. Close by is the **T'boli
Weaving Center**, where visitors can watch members of
this hill group produce traditional fabrics.

About 36km (21.5 miles) northwest of the city near
the town of Malagos and on the lower slopes of Mt Apo
is the **Philippine Eagle Nature Center**. Run by the
Philippine Eagle Foundation, the centre operates a captive breeding programme for this endangered bird.

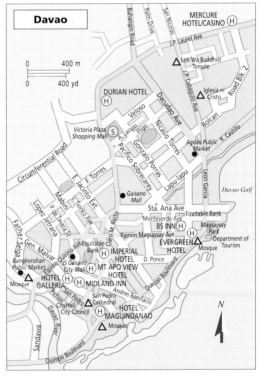

Success has been limited so far, only two off-spring being produced, but the place has a valuable role in introducing this magnificent bird to the public. Several eagles can be seen, living in huge cages that do give them, albeit limited, room to fly. The centre is laid out as a pleasant park that houses not just Philippine eagles but a variety of wildlife, including other endangered raptors and deer.

Off Davao's southeast coast lies **Samal Island**, the coast of which is dotted with beaches now being developed as Davao's resort. The island can be reached easily by a small but regular ferry from a wharf at Sasa, just to the north of the Insular Century Hotel Davao.

Mt Apo **

At 2954m (9689ft) Mt Apo is the Philippines' highest mountain, as well as being one of the country's largest and most important national parks. This is definitely the place for nature lovers. Most of its 720km^2 (260 sq miles) consists of dense rain forest providing home to many rare species of plants and animals unique to this country, including the Philippine eagle.

The climb to the summit is a challenging hike, along a steep but clear trail. Most hikers start at the town of **Kidapawan**, about two hours by bus west of Davao. From here, after collecting a permit from the municipal tourism council, located in the mayor's office, you take a jeepney to the village of **Lake Agco**, the end of the road and start of the trail. This is a beautiful spot, dense forest crowding around a steaming, bubbling volcanic lake, with a lodge and a campsite close by. Close to Lake Agco is a new geothermal plant, producing electricity for Davao. The Philippines has begun exploiting its volcanic geothermal sources in a big way and is already the world's second-biggest user of this energy source.

Do not attempt the climb without a guide. Engage one (and perhaps porters too) at Lake Agco and then start out early the next morning. The hike up takes 1½ days,

Above: *Enjoying a soak in the Lake Agco hot spring, on the slopes of Mt Apo.*

CLIMBING MT APO

Most climbers start and finish their hike at Lake Agco. First you have to pass through the entrance to a geothermal plant, and from here the path climbs over a hill and then steeply downhill to the Marbel River. The path follows the river, fording it many times, before leaving it and starting the real climb. The path from here is very steep and passes through dense forest for several hours. Eventually you reach a marshy plateau, the site of Lake Venado and the over-night campsite. Set off early next morning for the two-hour hike to the summit, initially pushing through tall cogon grass and later walking over open grasslands.

Right: *A small banca lies moored close to a stunning white beach on Santa Cruz Island, near Zamboanga.*
Opposite: *A vinta, a type of outrigger canoe renowned for its colourful sails, at Rio Hondo village, Zamboanga.*

with an overnight camp beside Lake Venado at 2400m (7872ft), and a day to return to Lake Agco. You will need to bring all your own kit, including tent and sleeping bags. Purchase your food in Davao or Kidapawan.

THE SOUTHWEST AND SULU

Taking in the Sulu Islands and the western peninsula of Mindanao, this area is close both physically and culturally to the Malaysian Islamic province of Sabah to the west. Throughout history outsiders have found it hard to rule the area – neither the Spanish nor the Americans succeeded – and today there is much resistance to rule from Christian Manila. This is the one region that still suffers from some security problems, with two Islamic separatist groups active and even piracy not uncommon. Nevertheless, this is an extremely beautiful region, and anyone who comes here will be treated to a quite unique aspect of the Philippines.

Zamboanga *

The capital of the southwest, Zamboanga is a largely Christian Filipino city in the midst of an otherwise Muslim region. In the city the old Spanish fort, **Fort Del Pilar**, houses the **Marine Life Museum**. Heading out of town to the northwest you come to **Pasonanca Park** and then **Climaco Freedom Park**, from where there is a good view of the city.

FIGHTING FOR MUSLIM AUTONOMY

Ever since the Spanish established a centralized Philippine state the Muslims of the far south have fought against it. To this day the people of Sulu and southwest Mindanao have proved difficult to handle, with – in recent years – three guerrilla groups fighting for autonomy or independence. Recently the largest group, the Moro National Liberation Front (MNLF), made a deal with the government that gave autonomy to the Islamic areas. To date, the much smaller Moro Islamic Liberation Front (MILF) and Abu Sayyaf groups have refused to make agreements and continue sporadic fighting and terrorist acts.

A few kilometres west of the city you encounter a **weaving village** run by Yakan people, one of the local ethnic groups, where fabrics made in traditional styles are manufactured and sold.

Tawi-Tawi **

These are the most southwesterly of the Sulu Islands and closer to Sabah than they are even to Zamboanga. Here people are wholly Malay and Islamic, Malaysian Ringgit circulate freely alongside Philippine Pesos, and the rule of Manila seems to have little meaning.

The capital of this group of 300 islands is **Bongao**, situated on a small island of the same name, to the southwest of the main Tawi-Tawi Island. There is an interesting, colourful market, and close to town one can climb 314m (1030ft) Mt Bongao. Some outer islets have fine beaches which can be visited. To the southwest lies **Sibutu**, the nearest significant Philippine island to Borneo. One of the main settlements here is **Sitangkai**, a town built on stilts in shallow water above a huge coral reef. It can be reached in a day trip by boat from Bongao.

AVOIDING TROUBLED AREAS

If travelling in western Mindanao and Sulu it is essential to follow advice on where it is and is not safe to go. Although the degree and locations of trouble vary, the main trouble spots in Mindanao are the Cotabato and Maguindanao provinces, where the MILF remains strong, and Zamboanga province where Abu Sayyaf carries out occasional terrorist acts and kidnappings. Abu Sayyaf is also very active in Basilan and parts of Sulu. Piracy is not uncommon throughout Sulu. If a local tells you that a certain locality is a no-go area, they mean it.

SULU AND THE CHINESE

Sulu is believed to have traded with China as far back as the 8th century, and to have had extensive dealings during the Song and Yuan dynasties (10th–14th centuries). Sulu exports to China included lacquer, beeswax, tortoise shells and pearls, the latter often as big as 2.5cm (1 inch) across. Sulu sent several envoys to China, and when China's foreign trade became state-controlled during the early part of the Ming dynasty (early 15th century), Sulu was a port of call for the first of the great imperial voyages made under the command of Zheng He.

Mindanao and Sulu at a Glance

Due to the complex effects of the northeast and southwest monsoons, the best times to visit vary quite considerably in different parts of Mindanao. Davao has a remarkably low rainfall, which remains steady throughout the year. Mt Apo is basically the same, though being a mountain it receives considerably more rain than Davao. Hikers should be prepared for rain at any time. Climbing the mountain is extremely popular during Holy Week, the week preceding Easter, so this would be a good time to avoid. Northern Mindanao receives most of its rain between November and January, and although there is no clearly defined dry season **March** to **May** are the driest months. The typhoon season (June–November) is the best time for surfers to be on Siargao. Camiguin has its annual Lanzones Festival in October, celebrating the harvest of this fruit, which is grown extensively there. The southwest has a short dry season in March and April; the highest rainfall occurs in October and November.

Daily **flights** and regular **ferries** connect Manila with Davao, Cagayan de Oro and Zamboanga. There are daily flights from Zamboanga to the Sulu Islands. Ferries ply this route but may not be entirely safe.
There are frequent high-speed **catamaran** ferries from Cagayan de Oro to Benoni, Camiguin's port. Regular slow ferries also link Benoni with Balingoan, the nearest mainland harbour. Mambajao has an airport, but services, usually from Cebu, are intermittent. To reach Siargao Island, a daily ferry runs from Surigao to the island's port, Dapa.

Jeepneys and **taxis** are plentiful in Davao, Cagayan de Oro and Zamboanga. In Surigao transport is by **motorized tricycles**. To reach Mt Apo from Davao, air-conditioned and ordinary **buses** run frequently to Kidapawan, from where a jeepney can be taken to Lake Agco. To travel between the different parts of Mindanao, frequent air-conditioned and ordinary buses ply all the main routes. In addition, there are **flights** between Davao and Zamboanga, and between Davao and Cagayan de Oro. On Camiguin and Siargao, use a jeepney or hired **motorbike**. In the Sulu Islands everyone uses a **boat**, either scheduled ferries or by special hire.

Davao
LUXURY
Insular Century Hotel Davao, Lanang, Davao City, tel: (082) 234-3050, fax: (082)
62959. Manila office: G/F, Hotel Intercontinental Manila, Ayala Ave, Makati, tel: (02) 815-1930. A modern hotel on the shore facing Samal Island. Extensive garden, a small golf course and a swimming pool.

MID-RANGE
Durian Hotel, JP Laurel Ave, Davao City, tel: (082) 221-8216, fax: (082) 221-2835. A largish city hotel, with air-conditioned rooms.
Villa Margarita, JP Laurel Ave, Davao City, tel: (082) 221-5674, fax: (082) 62928. A pleasant, small hotel, built in a Spanish villa style.

Camiguin Island
MID-RANGE
Paras Beach Resort, Yumbing, Mambajao, Camiguin Island, tel: (088) 879-008. A beachside development at the northern tip of the island, with air-conditioned rooms, restaurant and a swimming pool. Diving facilities are available.

BUDGET
Caves Resort, Agoho, Mambajao, Camiguin Island, tel: (088) 879-040, fax: (088) 870-077. A popular beachside resort, located at the northern end of the island. Consists of rooms on stilts built right up to the edge of the beach, plus cottages built further back in a coconut palm grove. The resort has its own restaurant and diving facilities.

Mindanao and Sulu at a Glance

Siargao Island
BUDGET
Boyum's Cove Surf Camp, Cloud Nine, General Luna, Siargao Island, Surigao del Norte. Simple bungalows set among coconut palms, on the shore in a small cove with mangroves. The restaurant here is the only place to eat.

Zamboanga
LUXURY
Lantaka Hotel by the Sea, Valderrosa St, Zamboanga, tel: (062) 991-2033, fax: (062) 991-1626. A spacious hotel set in its own garden. Rooms are air-conditioned, with balconies and a sea view.

WHERE TO EAT

Davao
Top of the Apo, Apo View Hotel, J Camus St, Davao City, tel: (082) 221-6430. International cuisine with a view of the city.
Orchid Café, Insular Century Hotel Davao, Lanang, Davao City, tel: (082) 234-3050. Dishes from across Asia.

Zamboanga
Alavar's House of Seafood, Justice Lim Boulevard, Zamboanga. Excellent seafood.

TOURS AND EXCURSIONS

The **Department of Tourism** in Davao can help arrange a tour of the southern Mindanao region, which includes making arrangements for a hike up Mt Apo.

The **Kidapawan Municipal Tourism Council** is also of great help. Indeed, anyone intending to climb Mt Apo via the Lake Agco route must first obtain a permit here. There are car hire companies in Davao, but only with chauffeur-driven cars: as with the Visayas, self-drive car hire is not an option.

The **Department of Tourism** in Zamboanga may be able to help with travel plans in the Sulu Islands, but for trips to Camiguin and Siargao Islands you will need to make your own arrangements.

SPORT

Diving facilities are still rather limited in Mindanao. However, dive operations have been set up on Samal Island, while on Camiguin Island a couple of resorts have facilities. The resorts on Siargao have snorkelling equipment for hire.
Hiking is well established on Mt Apo, and local **mountaineering** groups are attempting to set up trails on more of Mindanao's mountains. The Department of Tourism in Cagayan de Oro

may be able to help with arrangements to climb Mt Kitanglad. Davao has three **golf** courses. Two of them are full 18-hole courses and one is a 9-hole course.
Surfers heading for Siargao Island need to be self-sufficient in kit. There are no facilities to hire, buy or repair surf boards.

USEFUL CONTACTS

Department of Tourism, Region XI, Door no 7, Magsaysay Park Complex, Sta Ana District, Davao City, tel: (082) 221-6955, fax: (082) 221-0070.
Department of Tourism, Region X, A Velez St, Cagayan de Oro City, tel: (088) 856-4048, fax: (088) 723-696.
Department of Tourism, Region IX, Lantaka Hotel by the Sea, Valderrosa St, Zamboanga City, tel: (062) 991-0218, fax: (062) 991-0217.
Philippine Airlines, Davao Airport Ticket Office, tel: (082) 234-0073; Cagayan de Oro Airport Ticket Office, tel: (08822) 725-592.

DAVAO	J	F	M	A	M	J	J	A	S	O	N	D
AVERAGE TEMP. °F	81	81	81	82	82	82	81	81	81	82	82	81
AVERAGE TEMP. °C	27	27	27	28	28	28	27	27	27	28	28	27
RAINFALL ins.	4.7	4.2	3.3	5.7	17.4	7.5	6	6.8	7.2	6.8	5.2	3.8
RAINFALL mm	119	107	85	145	189	189	154	175	181	174	131	98
DAYS OF RAINFALL	13	12	11	11	16	18	15	14	15	15	14	13

8
Palawan

The third-largest of the Philippine islands, this long sliver of land has been dubbed the country's last frontier. Its 11,785 km² (4550 sq miles), comprising 1768 islands, are home to only 700,000 people, and despite rapid population growth the region is still rich in tracts of forest. Wildlife abounds, including numerous species of bird and mammal that live nowhere else. So important is Palawan to Southeast Asian conservation that in 1990 UNESCO declared the whole of Palawan a Man and the Biosphere Reserve.

Visitors come to Palawan almost solely for its natural beauty. Protected areas are high on the list of places to visit, as are some of the many hundreds of islands, where resorts offer the chance to play at Robinson Crusoe.

The northern parts of Palawan are most easily reached by plane from Manila. The most famous of these places are **Bacuit Bay** and the little town of **El Nido**, site of a cluster of limestone islands complete with towering peaks and dizzying cliffs. Further north the **Calamian** group of islands includes **Coron Island**, where the highly endangered Philippine cockatoo can still be seen, **Coron Bay**, which is rapidly becoming a new mecca for wreck diving, and **Calauit Island**, a wildlife sanctuary that has become a natural home to several species of African mammals.

Further south, **St Paul's Underground River National Park** is reachable from provincial capital **Puerto Princesa**. Most isolated of all, **Tubbataha Reef**, a major attraction to divers, is a nine-hour boat journey from the city.

DON'T MISS

*** **El Nido:** sheer cliffs and isolated beaches.
*** **St Paul's Underground River National Park:** a river flowing in a limestone cave.
*** **Sabang:** a truly spectacular beach.
*** **Calauit Island:** a safari with African wildlife.
*** **Tubbataha Reef:** exciting underwater life.
** **Crocodile Farming Institute:** get really close to a lot of crocodiles.
** **Coron Island:** visit the stunning inland lake.
** **Coron Bay:** one of Asia's best wreck diving sites.

Opposite: *Cottages of the Miniloc Island Resort, Miniloc Island, El Nido.*

Above: *A small river lined with mangroves cuts through the shore at the eastern end of Sabang Beach, demarcating the edge of the forest in St Paul's Underground River National Park.*

CENTRAL PALAWAN

This is the narrow waist of the province, where in places the island is barely 10km (6 miles) wide. It is the most populated and developed part of Palawan, and the home of Puerto Princesa, the provincial capital. Though this area has more cleared land than almost anywhere else in Palawan, there is still much rugged, forested terrain, notably **Cleopatra's Needle**, at 1593m (5225ft) the highest mountain in central Palawan, as well as the highly protected area of St Paul's Underground River National Park. Between Puerto Princesa City and St Paul's is island-studded **Honda Bay**, a pretty area with a few beaches and some good snorkelling that can be visited by boat from the city.

Puerto Princesa *

Established as recently as 1970, the municipality of Puerto Princesa is huge, covering much of central Palawan, and making it the second-largest municipal area in the Philippines, after Davao. The total population, however, is only 120,000, and the city itself is quite small, if rather sprawling. It has a reputation as the cleanest city in the Philippines, the result of rigorously enforced laws introduced by the environmentally conscious city government. Even tricycles have ashtrays!

The heart of the city is Rizal Avenue, running east–west for 3km (2 miles) from near the port to the airport. Most of the city's main buildings are laid out along or near this road, including the market, shops, banks, museum, government buildings and many of the hotels.

There are few specific sights within the city, apart from the **Palawan Museum**, situated next to Mendoza Park. As can be expected, it chronicles the history and describes the people of Palawan. Just outside the urban area, at Irawan, a few kilometres north of the city, is the **Crocodile Farming Institute**, a place that aims through research to conserve the two species of Philippine crocodiles. The institute houses a large number of crocodiles and is also home to a small collection of other species of Palawan wildlife, the result of illegally caught animals confiscated by police. Guided tours are available every afternoon (13:00–16:30 daily). Beyond Irawan, continuing along the road towards Aborlan to the south of Puerto Princesa, is the **Iwahig Prison and Penal Colony**. Not exactly the kind of place one would normally visit, Iwahig is a prison without bars, where the convicts work in the open fields. Handicrafts made by the convicts can even be bought at the prison's own handicraft store.

CROCODILES

The **Crocodile Farming Institute**, just outside Puerto Princesa, was set up with Japanese funding to find ways to protect the Philippines' two species of crocodile, the saltwater and Philippine crocodiles. Research has gone into environmental conservation, farming techniques and ways to improve the animals' rather negative image with the public. Work is ongoing, and visitors are able to undertake free tours of some of the breeding pens, as well as a natural habitat containing a number of crocodiles.

Below: *Visitors viewing crocodiles captively bred at the Crocodile Farming Institute, Puerto Princesa.*

Below: *A guided tour
along the underground
river at St Paul's
Underground River.*

Sabang and St Paul's Underground River ***

Approximately 80km (50 miles) north of the urban area
of Puerto Princesa, but still within the municipality, lies
central Palawan's principal visitor attraction, St Paul's
Underground River National Park. Here a river runs for
8km (5 miles) through a limestone cave before opening
into a lagoon that is separated from the sea only by a low
sandbar. The whole area is surrounded by protected rain
forest, above which stands the 1028m (3372ft) dome-
shaped peak of Mt St Paul's, named in the 19th century
by British sailors for its apparent resemblance to St
Paul's Cathedral in London.

Access from Puerto Princesa is by a rough road to
Sabang, a tiny village with one of Palawan's most magnificent beaches. It is worth making a trip to Sabang for
the beach alone. At Sabang, you can either walk to the
national park along the beach and then through rain
forest, a distance of about 4km (2.5 miles), or hire a boat
for the 15-minute ride. Entry permits are essential, available either at the national park office in Puerto Princesa,
or at the small office in Sabang.

The boat ride takes you to a beach from where it is a
200m (219yd) walk through forest to the check-in desk,
where permits are checked and boats arranged. Small
outrigger boats equipped with powerful lamps take
visitors into the underground river, upstream for 1km
(0.6 mile) to the inner end of the 'Highway', a long and

Left: *A group of Moorish idols swim past a soft coral clinging to a rocky wall, close to Bird Island, in the north of Tubbataha Reef Marine National Park.*

perfectly straight stretch of high-roofed tunnel, before turning around and returning. Many areas have fascinating stalactites and stalagmites, and one is constantly surrounded by the twitching noises of thousands of bats and swiftlets.

Outside the cave the forest teems with wildlife, especially Philippine macaques and monitor lizards, and is worth exploring. Around the picnic area close to the beach, Tabon birds can frequently be seen. This highly endangered flightless bird thrives at St Paul's. One of its unique features is the enormous mound of sand that it builds over its eggs.

TUBBATAHA REEF

Lying 150km (95 miles) southeast of Puerto Princesa, this 33,200ha (120 sq mile) reef is a marine national park with a huge diversity of coral and fish living on and around it. Consisting of two atolls, each with their own small islands, the reef is also breeding ground for several species of maritime bird, especially boobies and noddies.

The reef is a diver's paradise, with virtually everything known to exist in the seas around the Philippines available here, from the tiniest corals and reef fish to sharks, turtles and manta rays. Its isolation and usually rough seas have helped protect it, and the only access is via live-aboard dive cruises that visit this area during the March–May calm season. These dive ships usually operate out of either Puerto Princesa or Iloilo.

THE IMPORTANCE OF TUBBATAHA REEF

Tubbataha consists of two coral atolls, each with a small islet surrounded by extensive reefs, and separated by a channel 8km (5 miles) wide. The nearest human settlement is a seaweed farm on Arena Reef, about 80km (50 miles) to the northeast. Traditionally, the reef has been protected from human interference for 9 months of the year by rough seas, but over the past decade **dynamite** fishing has been conducted through much of the year. Protection of the reef is essential not only for its own beauty but also because it is believed to supply a very large proportion of the fish fry that eventually migrate all round Palawan, sustaining the entire province's fishing industry.

Right: *A fishing village adjacent to the town of Taytay, seen from the walls of an old Spanish fort. Situated in the north of Palawan, Taytay was once the provincial capital. Today, it is a rather remote, sleepy town.*

NORTHERN PALAWAN

This is one of the remotest regions of the Philippines. Much of it remains densely forested, though many areas are being rapidly cleared as settlers move in. The roads are rough and public transport unreliable. Boats are often the best way to get around, and the whole region is generally better accessed from Manila, via the airport at **El Nido**, than by road from Puerto Princesa.

In the south, places of interest include the small beach resort of **Port Barton** on the west coast, while close to the town of Roxas on the east coast is the resort island of **Coco-Loco**. To the north is the town of **Taytay**, which is the access point for the **Club Noah Isabelle** resort, while further north still lies **El Nido**, one of the gems of the Philippines.

Taytay *

Taytay, once the capital of Palawan, lies on the northeast coast about 150km (95 miles) north of Puerto Princesa. The town itself is a quiet little place, its only specific site of interest being the ruins of an 18th-century Spanish **fort** built beside the harbour. The ruined walls were made from local coral. Offshore are numerous islands, which can be reached by hiring a boat at Taytay. Some of the islands have small resorts, most importantly **Apulit Island**, site of Club Noah Isabelle, an exclusive resort that claims to have a strong commitment to sustainable ecotourism. West of Taytay is **Malampaya Sound**, a vast enclosed bay that connects with Palawan's west coast. Malampaya Sound is so rich in marine life that it has become one of the Philippines' major fishing and fish farming grounds.

El Nido and Bacuit Bay ***

Situated 50km (30 miles) north of Taytay, this is one of the most beautiful spots in the Philippines. The bay contains a large number of islands, most characterized by towering limestone cliffs that are essentially a marine version of the famous karst limestone peaks of southern China. Some of the shorelines are marked by stunning beaches, while many of the less precipitous island slopes are covered with fragments of rain forest, home to hornbills, monkeys and monitor lizards.

El Nido town lies at the northern end of the area, itself in a dramatic setting, located on a sweeping sandy bay backed by sheer cliffs. It is a small place with hardly any traffic, apart from a few jeepneys that link the town to Taytay and Puerto Princesa. El Nido town has plenty of inexpensive accommodation and numerous restaurants, with several more resorts spread out along the coast further south at Corong-Corong.

> **ETHNIC GROUPS**
>
> The great majority of Palawan's inhabitants are immigrants from other parts of the Philippines, especially the Visayas. Inward migration is causing the population to grow by 4 per cent annually, greatly threatening the natural environment. The original inhabitants, now very much a minority in their own land, are the Tagbanua, the Pala'wan, Batak, Tau't Batu and Jama Mapun. Some of these are being assimilated into Filipino society, but others still live a primitive existence in the forests. Another minority group, though immigrants from · Sulu, are the Badjao – the Sea Gypsies – who spend their entire lives on the water.

Left: *Vertical limestone cliffs tower above the township of El Nido, principal settlement in Bacuit Bay. Situated in a very remote area of north-western Palawan, the immense beauty of the island-studded bay was only discovered by the outside world in the early 1990s. Now, with its own small airport and daily flights to and from Manila, El Nido is the latest must-see beauty spot.*

ECO-FRIENDLY
DEVELOPMENT?

With much concern for the
protection of Palawan's
natural environment, but
taking into account its
obvious tourist potential,
developers have tried to
bring in ecotourism through
environmentally friendly
resorts. New resorts all
attempt to emphasize their
developers' commitment to
the environment, with efforts
to limit impact on surrounding forests, beaches and
reefs, to help protect known
indigenous species, and to
minimize waste and the drain
on local resources, as well as
to generate employment for
the inhabitants. But materials
must all come from some-
where and in the quest for
profits some corners have
been cut. Visitors to such
resorts are asked to watch
out for and report any less
than eco-friendly practices.

Below: *Miniloc Island
Resort, nestling in its own
cove and surrounded by
sheer limestone cliffs.*

El Nido town is a pleasant place to relax, but the main
attraction has to be the islands. Boats can be hired to
make leisurely tours around almost any of the islands (a
couple are closed due to the presence of the military), or
simply to ferry you to and from a beach of your choice.
The boatmen all know the best spots. There are
a number of good snorkelling sites, and for divers
there are several dive operators based in El Nido town.
Unfortunately, although the snorkelling is very good,
with excellent corals in the shallow waters, at greater
depths dynamite fishing has caused extensive damage,
and good corals exist only in patches. Nevertheless, there
is plenty of interesting marine life; turtles, for example,
can be seen frequently.

One of the most interesting islands for a tour is
Miniloc, where two lagoons, both ringed by sheer limestone cliffs, can be explored. Here the scenery is stunning
and the water crystal clear. Turtles frequently use these
sheltered waters, and there have even been occasional
reports of whales entering the larger lagoon. Close to
Miniloc is one of the symbols of El Nido – the **Très
Marias**, an islet consisting of three jagged slabs of rock
pointing upwards from the water's surface. It is immediately around this islet that some of the best snorkelling
can be found.

For those who want to experience island life at close
quarters, several islands have resorts, most notably
Malapacao, Langen and Miniloc islands. The last
two have truly luxuri-
ous resorts owned by
a company called Ten
Knots. The one set on
Langen Island, called
(strangely enough)
Lagen Island Resort,
is flanked by enor-
mous cliffs and set
against dense forest
that is well worth
exploring.

CALAMIAN ISLANDS

The Calamian Islands are the most northerly part of Palawan, and consist mainly of Busuanga, Coron, Culion and Calauit islands. The main town and focus for visitors is **Coron**, situated confusingly on Busuanga Island.

Unlike most of Palawan, many of the islands, with the exception of Coron Island, have been deforested, and have at best patches of scrub. A large part of Busuanga Island is given over to what is claimed to be Asia's largest cattle ranch.

Coron Town and Coron Bay **

Coron town is a small, friendly place that stretches along the shoreline at the eastern end of Coron Bay. Behind the town rises **Mt Dapias**, recently topped with a satellite television receiver. It is well worth climbing this hill for its superb view across the bay and **Coron Island**. Just to the east of town is **Makinit Hot Spring**, consisting of a pleasant hot pool close to the shore. It can be reached by taking a tricycle to the end of the road and then walking for about 20 minutes along the shore.

Above: *The view from Mt Dapias across Coron Bay, to the cliffs of Coron Island.*

PALAWAN WILDLIFE

Although Palawan's wildlife is similar to that of Borneo, there are species unique to this island. These include the Palawan peacock pheasant, and Palawan hornbill. Both are highly endangered despite the survival of the forest. Other animals found in both Palawan and Borneo include the scaly anteater, Asian short-clawed otter, mouse deer and porcupine. The waters around Palawan are home to endangered species such as the hawksbill, green and Olive Ridley turtles, and the dugong, or sea cow.

Above: *A Japanese wartime wreck in Coron Bay, Calamian Islands.*

JAPANESE WRECKS

Coron Bay is littered with the wrecks of Japanese ships sunk by US aircraft in 1944. To date 12 wrecks have been found, some of which are now regularly dived. All are about a two-hour boat ride from Coron town, located in the western part of the bay. They include the *Taiei Maru*, a 10,000-tonne tanker in 26m (85ft) of water; the *Akitsu-shima*, a warship lying 38m (125ft) down; and the *Olympia Maru* and *Kogyo Maru*, both freighters lying on their side 25m (80ft) and 34m (110ft) down respectively. Most have extensive coral growth over them, and are home to a lot of fish, including lionfish and the dangerous scorpionfish.

Many houses in Coron are built on stilts over the water. This is especially true on the eastern edge of town where a whole village of **Badjao** fisherfolk live. The result, though picturesque, has rendered this part of Coron Bay far from pristine. Swimming close to the town is definitely not recommended!

Coron town is the local headquarters for several diving operations, as the area is slowly becoming a major wreck diving centre. The wrecks are the result of a World War II air raid by US aircraft on a fleet of Japanese supply ships that had hidden among the islands of Coron Bay. Various ships have been identified and surveyed, mostly around **Tangat Island**, about two hours by boat west of Coron town. Many of the wrecks are still surprisingly intact, with their cargoes still clearly visible. Marine life around them is extensive, corals growing well on the hulls and fish making good use of the many nooks and crannies. Being a largely enclosed bay, underwater visibility is bad, but for those interested in wrecks this is one of the best sites in Southeast Asia.

Coron Island **

To the south of Coron town lies Coron Island, a place of jagged limestone peaks, rather like El Nido but forming one solid land mass. It is a mysterious place, whose inhabitants, members of the Tagbanua ethnic group, have gone to some pains to protect their environment and keep outsiders away. As a result, the less rocky areas are covered with rain forest, where the endangered Philippine cockatoo can still be seen. The entire island was recently declared a protected area.

The island also has numerous freshwater lakes, which are sacred to the Tagbanua. Only one is accessible: **Lake Kayangan**, situated on the northwestern side of the island. A boat trip from Coron town will take you to a lagoon on the west coast, from where it is a short hike to the lake. The eastern side of the island, facing the open sea and site of the Tagbanua's two villages, is out of bounds due to the islanders' reluctance to accept visitors.

Calauit Island ★★★

At the far northwestern end of Busuanga Island lies
Calauit Island, separated from its larger neighbour only
by a large mangrove swamp. Back in 1976, as the last
stronghold of the Calamian deer, a locally endemic animal, the island was designated a wildlife sanctuary. In
1977, then-president and dictator Marcos ordered all the
island's inhabitants to move out, replacing them with
eight species of African mammals and thereby creating
one of Asia's most remarkable safari parks.

Today, despite attempts by the former inhabitants to
return, the sanctuary still exists and most of the African
mammals and Philippine wildlife are thriving. In those
extensive areas where the African animals are allowed to
roam at will they have moulded the landscape into a
savannah. Herds of giraffe, zebra, impala, waterbuck
and eland can easily be seen, along with large numbers
of the resurgent Calamian deer and many birds.

Above: *A view across the
town of Coron and the
sheltered waters of Coron
Bay.*
Left: *A herd of eland, a
species of African antelope,
wanders through savan-
nah-like grassland in
Calauit Island Wildlife
Sanctuary, off the north-
western tip of Busuanga
Island.*

Palawan at a Glance

Palawan is hot and humid all year, and from mid-May to the end of December is rainy too. Unpaved roads turn to mud and become impassable. The only dry period is **January** to early **May**, when roads are dry and dusty but usable.

Puerto Princesa is reached by direct daily **flights** from Manila, and indirectly via Manila from Cebu and other centres. Northern Palawan can be reached by daily flights from Manila to El Nido. The Calamian Islands are served by daily flights from Manila to Busuanga Airport. Tubbataha Reef is accessible only by **cruise boat** from Puerto Princesa or Iloilo. **Ferries** connect Puerto Princesa with Manila, Iloilo, Bacolod and Cebu, and Coron with Manila and Batangas.

Jeepneys and one air-conditioned **minibus** link Sabang with Puerto Princesa daily. **Buses** leave Puerto Princesa each morning at 07:00 to go to Roxas and Taytay. One jeepney per day, leaving at 07:00, goes from Taytay to El Nido, but this is usually over-crowded and breakdowns are frequent. Instead, go to nearby Agpay and hire a **boat** to El Nido. A **ferry** links Sabang and El Nido twice a week. Ferries link Coron town with Taytay and Liminancong (near

El Nido). Calauit Island can be reached from Coron town by one daily bus that leaves at 09:00–10:00. It starts the return journey from Quezon, the village on Busuanga nearest to Calauit at 02:00 (2 o'clock in the morning)! Alternatively, boats can be hired. The journey takes six hours one way.

Puerto Princesa
LUXURY
Asiaworld Resort Hotel Palawan, San Miguel, Puerto Princesa, tel: (048) 433-2212, fax: (048) 433-2111. Modern hotel in gardens with pool.

MID-RANGE
Badjao Inn, 350 Rizal Ave, Puerto Princesa, tel: (048) 433-2761, fax: (048) 433-2180, e-mail: badjao@pal-onl.com. Pleasant rooms around a quadrangle containing a garden and open restaurant.
Casa Linda Inn, Trinidad Rd, Puerto Princesa, tel: (048) 433-2606, fax: (048) 433-2309. Pleasant rooms and garden.

Sabang
BUDGET
Robert's Cottages, Sabang, Cabayugan, Puerto Princesa City, tel: (048) 433-4161. Beach-front cottages among coconut palms, restaurant.

Taytay
LUXURY
Club Noah Isabelle, Apulit Island, Taytay. Manila booking

address: 2/F Basic Petroleum Building, C. Palanca Jr St, Legaspi Village, Makati City 1229, Metro Manila, tel: (02) 810-7291, fax: (02) 818-2640. A luxurious resort complex in a stunning setting, complete with coral reef and rain forest.

BUDGET
Pem's Pension House and Restaurant, Mr Pempe de Luna, Taytay. Simple rooms and bungalows beside the harbour, with one of the town's very few restaurants.

El Nido
LUXURY
Miniloc Island Resort and **Lagen Island Resort**, El Nido. Manila office: Ten Knots Development Corporation, 2/F Builders Centre Building, 170 Salcedo St, Legaspi Village, Makati City 1229, Metro Manila, tel: (02) 894-5644, fax: (02) 810-3620. Modern, luxurious resorts in island settings with beaches and forest.

MID-RANGE
Dolarog Beach Resort, Dolarog, El Nido. A self-contained resort on the coast south of El Nido town.

BUDGET
Lally and Abet Beach Cottages, El Nido. A collection of bungalows beside the beach, with own restaurant, on the very edge of El Nido town but only a short walk into the centre. Lovely view of the bay.

Palawan at a Glance

Calamian Islands
LUXURY
Club Paradise, Dimakya Island, Busuanga. Manila booking address: Euro-Pacific Resorts Inc, Building IV, Celery Rd, FTI Complex, Taguig, Metro Manila, tel: (02) 838-4956, fax: (02) 838-4462, e-mail: clubpara@pworld.net.ph, website: http://clubpar.com. A self-contained luxury resort on its own island off the north coast of Busuanga.

BUDGET
Sea Breeze Lodge, Coron, fax: (02) 804-0331. Built on piles out over the water, with its own restaurant, and one of Coron's best dive operations.

WHERE TO EAT
Puerto Princesa
Café Kamarikutan, Rizal Ave Extension, tel: (048) 433-5182. Bamboo building, serves Filipino dishes.
Pink Lace, Rizal Ave, tel: (048) 433-2168. Serves Vietnamese, Filipino and Indian cuisine.
Pho Vietnamese, Valencia St, tel: (048) 433-3576. Vietnamese food.

El Nido
Ric Sons, Calle Hama, El Nido. A lovely view over the bay; serves a range of dishes.

TOURS AND EXCURSIONS
Getting around Palawan can be difficult, time-consuming and tiring. There are several travel agencies who can

arrange some or all of your transport. Most are based in Puerto Princesa, though they may have branches in Coron and El Nido, and some have offices in Manila too.

SPORT
By far the most important sport for visitors to Palawan is **diving**. Although some reefs have been damaged by dynamite and cyanide fishing, many are still in pristine condition. Dive operations are based in Puerto Princesa, El Nido, Coron town, Club Paradise and Club Noah Isabelle. Trips can be organized either upon arrival at your destination, or in Manila, using one of several companies that specialize in diving. You must arrange live-aboard cruises to Tubbataha Reef in advance through a Manila dive specialist as places are limited. Other water sports include **yacht** charter and **kayaking**, both recently introduced in Coron town. **Trekking** can also be arranged, for example to climb Cleopatra's Needle. Always take a guide. Make arrangements through a travel agent in Puerto Princesa.

Philippine Airlines, Puerto Princesa Airport, Rizal Ave Extension, Puerto Princesa, tel: (048) 433-4565.

USEFUL CONTACTS
Provincial Tourism Division, Ground Floor, Capitol Building Complex, Rizal Ave, Puerto Princesa, tel: (048) 433-2968.
City Tourism Office, Airport Compound, Puerto Princesa, tel: (048) 433-2983.
WG & A Superferry, Aboitiz Air Transport Corporation, Rizal Ave, Puerto Princesa, tel: (048) 433-4875.
Go Palawan Travel and Tours, Rizal Ave, Puerto Princesa, tel: (048) 433-4570, fax: (048) 433-4580. Ticketing and arrangement of Palawan transportation. Runs a daily air-conditioned minibus to Sabang.
Island Divers Ventures, 371 Rizal Ave, Puerto Princesa, tel: (048) 433-2917. Dive operation specializing in Palawan diving.
Sea Dive Center, Coron, fax: (02) 804-0331. Dive centre based at Sea Breeze resort in Coron, concentrating on wreck diving in Coron Bay.

PUERTO PRINCESA	J	F	M	A	M	J	J	A	S	O	N	D
AVERAGE TEMP. °F	81	81	81	82	82	82	81	81	81	81	81	81
AVERAGE TEMP. °C	27	27	27	29	29	28	27	27	27	27	27	27
RAINFALL ins.	1	0.6	0.9	1.4	5.2	7	7	6.6	7.3	8.2	8.1	4.6
RAINFALL mm	27	15	23	36	131	177	176	167	186	208	206	117
DAYS OF RAINFALL	4	2	3	5	11	15	17	17	16	17	14	9

Travel Tips

Tourist Information

Department of Tourism, overseas offices:

Australia: Highmount House, Level 6, 122 Castlereagh St, Sydney, tel: (02) 267-2695, fax: 283-1862.

Hong Kong: 6/F United Centre, 95 Queensway, tel: 2866-7652, fax: 2866-6521.

UK: 146-148 Cromwell Rd, London, SW7 4EF, tel: (020) 7835-1100, fax: 7835-1926.

Germany: Kaiser Strasse 15, Frankfurt, tel: (069) 20893, fax: 285127.

USA: 556 Fifth Avenue, New York, NY10036, tel: (212) 575-7915, fax: 302-6759.

Head office: Department of Tourism, DOT Building, TM Kalaw St, Ermita, Manila, tel: (02) 524-2345, fax: 521-8321.

Local offices:

Cordillera Administrative Region: DOT-Complex, Gov. Pack Rd, Baguio City, tel: (074) 442-8848, fax: 442-8848.

Regional Office V: Regional Centre Site, Rawis, Legaspi City, Albay, tel: (052) 482-0712, fax: 482-0811.

Regional Office VI: Western Visayas Tourism Center, Capitol Ground, Bonifacio Drive, Iloilo City, tel: (033) 337-5411, fax: 335-0245.

Regional Office VII: G/F LDM Building, Lapu-Lapu St, Cebu City, tel: (032) 254-2811, fax: 254-2711.

Regional Office XI: Door No 7, Magsaysay Park Complex, Sta Ana, Davao City, tel: (082) 221-6955, fax: 221-0070.

Entry Requirements

All visitors require a passport that is valid for at least six months after the intended end of their stay in the Philippines. Travellers from almost all countries can stay in the Philippines for up to 21 days without a visa provided they have a return or onward plane ticket. This period can be extended by application for a visa for a stay of 59 days. Visas for 59-day stays can also be obtained in advance from the consular section of Philippine embassies. These can be for single or multiple entries. These visas can be further extended in the Philippines by application to the Commission of Immigration and Deportation. Many travel agencies can handle the paperwork.

Customs

Passing through Philippine customs is a painless process, with incoming passengers filling in a form before arrival, which is then handed to a customs official after immigration. There are no customs formalities when leaving the country. Those caught with illegal drugs face the death penalty.

Health Requirements

A yellow fever vaccination certificate is required for travellers arriving in the Philippines from an infected area.

Getting There

By Air: Philippine Airlines (PAL) is the national carrier, but in mid-1998 it closed down all its European and Australian operations. This airline now serves only Asian and North American destinations. Most Asian capital cities and a number of North American cities have direct services to the main international airport, Ninoy Aquino International Airport, in Manila. Passengers coming from Hong Kong, Tokyo, Malaysia and Singapore can also fly to Mactan International Airport in

Cebu. There are flights from Malaysia and Singapore to Davao. For those coming from Europe, most European airlines and many Asian airlines fly indirectly to Manila.

By Ferry: The only international ferry links are between the Malaysian province of Sabah and the Sulu Islands in the far south.

What to Pack

The Philippines is a tropical country so those visitors intending to stay close to sea level need bring only light clothing. A pullover or light jacket is advisable for air-conditioned buildings. Anyone travelling into the mountains will need heavier clothing. In Baguio, temperatures are pleasantly cool even in the daytime, and at night only a pullover or jacket is needed even in January. Those intending to climb mountains will need extensive clothing and all their own camping equipment. Surfers should bring their own boards and repair kits; facilities are still few and far between. Divers need bring only themselves and their license. This sport is well organized with just about every dive operation able to hire out kit. Everyone should bring sunblock, insect repellent and a hat. For photographers, print film is widely available, but slides are not. Lithium and longlife alkaline batteries are hard to find outside Manila.

Money Matters

Currency: The Philippine Peso is not a fully convertible international currency, so you are unlikely to be able to buy any before departure from your country, or to sell any after returning. Inflation is not a serious problem and though the Peso's value has slipped about 40 per cent against the US Dollar and Pound Sterling in the last couple of years, it has held up reasonably well compared to some other Asian currencies.

The Peso is divided into 100 Centavos, with coins at 1, 5, 25 and 50 Centavos, 1 and 5 Pesos. Notes are available as 5, 10, 20, 50, 100, 500 and 1000 Pesos.

Exchange: Facilities in Manila are extensive, with banks, hotels, money changers and many shops (especially department stores) changing foreign currency. The rates vary enormously, the best usually being offered by the money changers. Many Manila banks have ATMs that accept credit and Cirrus cards. Outside Manila and big cities exchange facilities are often limited to branches of the Philippine National Bank. As a result, exchange rates get worse the further you go from Manila.

Exchange facilities are very limited in Palawan, outside Puerto Princesa. Unlike most countries, even banks give a poorer exchange rate for traveller's cheques than cash. Banks are open 09:00–15:00 Mon–Fri. Money changers are open every day until late in the evening.

Credit cards: Most major credit cards are accepted in the cities and major tourist destinations. Credit cards are little used in Palawan.

Tipping: This is a widely expected part of life. Airports, ferry ports and bus stations are usually crawling with porters, who survive on what they are given by passengers in return for their help. In taxis it is normal to round up the fare.

Accommodation

In many of the major cities accommodation varies from simple pension houses up to five-star hotels. Away from the main cities and resorts, only cheaper hotels are likely to be available. Air-conditioning is available even in many very inexpensive hotels. Away from Manila, power cuts (called

CONVERSION CHART		
FROM	**TO**	**MULTIPLY BY**
Millimetres	Inches	0.0394
Metres	Yards	1.0936
Metres	Feet	3.281
Kilometres	Miles	0.6214
Square kilometres	Square miles	0.386
Hectares	Acres	2.471
Litres	Pints	1.760
Kilograms	Pounds	2.205
Tonnes	Tons	0.984
To convert Celsius to Fahrenheit: x 9 ÷ 5 + 32		

brownouts in the Philippines) and water shortages are common.

Eating Out

In Manila and Cebu City there is a vast choice, from Filipino rice dishes, to Japanese sushi, Chinese noodles, and American fastfood. Chinese restaurants are widespread, though often serving Filipino interpretations that bear little resemblance to the real thing. Filipino food consists mainly of rice dishes, with meat or fish and very few vegetables. In cities the widest choice of foods can be found in department stores or shopping malls. The best restaurants in small towns and minor cities are often those at the hotels.

Transport

Air: The Philippines has a comprehensive domestic air network that links Manila to most places. Flying between two points elsewhere in the country may entail first going to Manila and changing planes. The main carrier is Philippine Airlines (PAL), supplemented on many routes by a plethora of smaller airlines. PAL's domestic routes can be booked from overseas.

Ferries: An extensive network of ferries plies among the islands, ranging from large, comfortable ships, to *bancas*, outrigger boats fitted with an engine. Long distance ferries on the main intercity routes use large ships, operated by such companies as WG&A Lines, Sulpicio Lines and Negros Navigation. The fragmented islands of the Visayas used to take a long time to hop among, but recently a series of new high-speed catamaran services have been introduced, linking up Cebu, Ormoc, Tagbilaran, Cagayan de Oro, Dumaguete and Dipolog.

Trains: The rail network is very poor indeed. Within Manila a single line Light Rail Transit (LRT) runs north–south, and another is under construction that will make a loop around the city. For long distance trains, the country's one and only passenger line, which runs to the south of Luzon, has undergone a restoration and now links Manila with Legaspi in a 10-hour journey.

Buses: Ranging from luxurious air-conditioned to rickety tin can, thousands of buses ply the roads throughout the country. Comfort may not be guaranteed, but prices are always low. Most services set off in the morning, ensuring that destinations are reached by mid-afternoon.

Jeepneys: The uniquely Philippine jeepney serves as the ubiquitous form of local public transport, often taking over where the buses leave off. They ply the streets of large towns and cities, provide short-hop services among nearby towns and villages, and connect remote settlements in areas where the buses do not go. They can be uncomfortable, extremely crowded and slow, but a ride on one gives a true down-to-earth feel for the Philippines and its people.

Tricycles and pedicabs: Both three-wheelers – the former with an engine, the latter relying on pedal power – these are the taxis of most towns. They are inexpensive and very convenient, especially when carrying luggage.

Taxis: Manila's streets are clogged with taxis, and they are now spreading to many of the other major cities. They are usually air-conditioned, and inexpensive. Every taxi is metered, with a fixed flagfall and distance rates. It can be especially hard to persuade Manila taxi drivers to use the meter if you are carrying luggage, or if heading to or from the international airport. In Cebu City most taxi drivers refuse to use the meter to go anywhere on Mactan Island.

Car hire: In Manila, Cebu and some of Luzon's cities (such as Baguio and Subic Bay) self-drive car hire is available. Cars are usually in reasonable condition and come with full insurance. To hire one, present your own country's driving license (International Driving Licenses are generally not recognised). You will not be allowed to take a car on the car ferries that link Luzon and Cebu with the other islands. Hire rates are reasonable and fuel is inexpensive. However, driving on the Philippines' roads can be difficult, at least in part due to congestion and poor signposting.

Business Hours

Government offices and many private companies work either 08:00–17:00 or 09:00–18:00 Mon–Fri. Department stores and many shops are open 09:00 or 10:00 to 20:00 or 21:00 daily. Banks are open 09:00–15:00 Mon–Fri.

Time Difference

The Philippines is all in one time zone, GMT plus eight hours.

Communications

Opening times for post offices vary from place to place. Most are open about 08:00–17:00. Public telephones can be scarce, except in the major cities. In Manila most public phones are card-operated. In most other cities phones are coin-operated, taking one-Peso coins. Most city hotels provide reasonable telephone services, including international connections. Most towns and cities have telephone offices run by the Philippine Long Distance Telephone Company (PLDT) or Bayantel, where calls can be made at most times of the day or night. International phone calls are expensive, but it is seldom difficult to get a connection. Domestic calls are inexpensive, but it can be difficult to get through. Fax services are offered by the more expensive hotels and by the PLDT and Bayantel offices. E-mail services are growing rapidly across the country, with cybercafés becoming the rage. They are reasonably priced.

Electricity

The electricity supply is generally 220 volts, 60 cycles. However, a few places, notably the old American bases at Subic Bay, Clark and Baguio, have both 220 and 110 volt supplies. A confusing array of round, flat, two- and three-pin plugs is in use.

Weights and Measures

Officially the metric system is universal, but most Filipinos are equally at home with imperial units, happily mixing pounds,

kilos, feet and metres in their daily usage.

Health Precautions

Although the standard of hygiene in the Philippines is reasonable, cholera and other enteric diseases are present. It is advisable to be vaccinated against typhoid and to have a gammaglobulin injection against hepatitis A. Tap water is usually safe in Manila, especially at the higher class hotels, but one should drink bottled water. In country areas bottled water is available. **Malaria** is present in many

NUMBERS
One • isa
Two • dalawa
Three • tatlo
Four • apat
Five • lima
Six • anim
Seven • pito
Eight • walo
Nine • siyam
10 • sampu
11 • labing isa
12 • labing dal'wa
13 • labing tatlo
14 • labing apat
15 • labing lima
20 • dalawampu
21 • dalawamput isa
30 • tatlumpu
31 • tatlumput isa
40 • apatnapu
50 • limampu
60 • animnapu
70 • pitumpu
80 • walumpu
90 • siyamnapu
100 • isandaan
110 • isandaan sampu
200 • dalawandaan
300 • tatlondaan
1000 • libo
One million • angaw

areas below an altitude of
600m (2000ft), except Manila,
Bohol, Cebu, Leyte and
Catanduanes. The malignant
falciparum strain is present
and believed to be resistant to
chloroquine. Be sure to bring
the appropriate prophylactics
with you. Another mosquito-
borne disease is **Dengue
Fever**. Increasingly widespread, this viral disease loves
stagnant fresh water, especially in dirty conditions. There is
no treatment, except bed rest
and fever control. Avoid it by
ensuring protection from
mosquitoes.
Stagnant fresh water may also

be home to **Bilharzia** (schisto-
somiasis), so avoid swimming
in such pools, even if they
appear clean.
The above diseases are unlikely problems. Far more likely
are **dehydration**, **heat
stroke** and **sunburn**. Daytime
temperatures are usually over
30°C (86°F) with humidity at
about 95 per cent, so it is
advisable to take care.
Consume plenty of liquid and
do not be overactive in the
sun. To avoid sunburn, it is
important either to use sunblock or to keep most of your
body covered or in the shade.

Personal Safety

The Philippines has had an
image as a rather violent and
dangerous place. However,
insurgencies are mostly a thing
of the past, and while Filipino
men often look aggressive,
they are in fact almost always
kind and gentle.
Theft of property from hotel
rooms, buses and jeepneys
can be a problem. Many
hotels have safety deposit
boxes available. Attacks and
muggings are rare, and the
streets are generally safe at
any time. Women travelling
alone are prone to sexual

harassment, albeit usually
fairly mild.

Emergencies

Emergency numbers are not
the same throughout the
Philippines. In Manila dial 166
or (02) 523-8391 for the
police. In Davao dial 119 and
in Cebu (032) 71659. If
reporting a theft, be sure to
get a written report from the
police if you intend to make
an insurance claim once you
return home. The Department
of Tourism has an assistance
line on (02) 524-1703.

Etiquette

Filipinos are easy-going people. Nevertheless, an
understanding of a few basic
rules is important. Always be
polite and never lose your
temper, no matter how frus-
trating a situation may be.
Filipinos love to share, and so
if you are offered something,
perhaps something as simple
as a snack, it may be bad
manners to refuse, even if you
do so with good intentions.
Although no one will ever
complain, beach wear is
inappropriate for the town.
In Moslem areas women
should dress conservatively.

GOOD READING

Conrad, Joseph (1899) *Lord Jim,* Penguin.
Young, Gavin (1983) *Slow Boats to China,* Penguin.
Young, Gavin (1992) *In Search of Conrad,* Penguin.
Rizal, José, translated by Lacson-Locsin, Ma Soledad; edited by
Locsin, Raul (1997) *Noli Me Tangere,* University of Hawaii Press.
Bacho, Peter (1991) *Cebu,* University of Washington Press.
Berlow, Alan (1996) *Dead Season: A Story of Murder and Revenge
on the Philippine Island of Negros.* Pantheon.
José, F Sionil (1996) *Sins: A Novel,* Random House.
Hamilton-Patterson, James (1998) *America's Boy,* Granta.